Greek and
Roman Oratory

DOVER·THRIFT·EDITIONS

Greek and
Roman Oratory

Edited by Bob Blaisdell

DOVER PUBLICATIONS, INC.
Mineola, New York

DOVER THRIFT EDITIONS

GENERAL EDITOR: MARY CAROLYN WALDREP
EDITOR OF THIS VOLUME: JIM MILLER

Bibliographical Note

Greek and Roman Oratory is a new work, first published by
Dover Publications, Inc., in 2014.

International Standard Book Number

ISBN-13: 978-0-486-49622-1
ISBN-10: 0-486-49622-8

Manufactured in the United States by Courier Corporation
49622801   2014
www.doverpublications.com

Contents

NOTE

Never in my opinion would the founders of cities have
induced their unsettled multitudes to form communities
had they not moved them by the magic of their eloquence: never without the highest gifts of oratory would
the great legislators have constrained mankind to submit
themselves to the yoke of law. Nay, even the principles
which should guide our life, however fair they may be by
nature, yet have greater power to mold the mind to virtue, when the beauty of things is illumined by the splendor of eloquence.

—Quintilian, *The Institutio Oratoria*[1]

There are many good reasons to read the Greek and Roman clas-
sics, perhaps the first being the pleasure of being in the company of
ancient minds creating the modern mind. The past seems present.
In their histories and impromptu speeches we encounter all of our
familiar problems of negotiating social dynamics in the midst of
international politics or of justifying warfare. Despite the full com-
plement of shysters and criminals among the orators, the Greek and
Roman statesmen can make us wish our own politicians and think-
ers were as vigorous and intelligent, as incisive and bold. "When
oratory is considered in all its periods," wrote Guy Carleton Lee,
the compiler of a vast collection of the world's speeches, "it will be
found that although there are vestiges of eloquence in the sacred
writings of the Hebrews, and various manifestations of the divine
gift among other great nations of ancient times, yet it was among
the Greeks that public speech as an art took its origin, had its

---

[1]Marcus Fabius Quintilianus. *The Institutio Oratoria of Quintilian*. Translated by
H. E. Butler. London: William Heineman. 1933.

development, and attained its acme; and in the period of its perfect flower produced the models of eloquence for all succeeding statesmen and orators."[2]

I have assembled over twenty speeches here that for the most part are famous less for their effect on events of the time than for the elation readers ever after have felt as they reimagine these situations in which various leaders attempt to raise spirits or turn a tide. There are orators we appreciate as heroes (e.g. Pericles, Socrates, Demosthenes, Cicero) as well as those we pity as villains; for example, our sympathetic understanding of the dastardly Catiline results from our appreciation of his chutzpah and recklessness of purpose, his impending doom. We can enjoy slippery Alcibiades irresistibly advocating for Athens' mistaken and fateful assault on Sicily.

The men who recorded or recreated or reimagined these speeches were geniuses of expression. Quintilian, who ran an ancient school of rhetoric, reflects: "Is it not a noble thing, by employing the understanding which is common to mankind and the words that are used by all, to win such honor and glory that you seem not to speak or plead, but rather, as was said of Pericles, to thunder and lighten?"[3] What was fresh to the orators and their audiences remains fresh today.

Thucydides, "a writer whose mind makes an overwhelming impression on his reader,"[4] in his *History of the Peloponnesian War*, is the source for several of the speeches; he remains for some of us the ideal historian, a participant in and intense recorder of the events he describes and relates, continually reminding himself and us that his work is not one of fancy or wish-fulfillment, but rigorous research: "As to the speeches which were made either before or during the war, it was hard for me, and for others who reported them to me, to recollect the exact words. I have therefore put into the mouth of each speaker the sentiments proper to the occasion, expressed as

---

[2]Guy Carleton Lee. *Orators of Ancient Greece*. New York: G.P. Putnam's Sons. 1900.

[3]Marcus Fabius Quintilianus. *The Institutio Oratoria of Quintilian*. Translated by H. E. Butler. London: William Heineman. 1933.

[4]H. D. F. Kitto. *The Greeks*. Harmondsworth, England: Penguin. 1973. 138. Kitto adds: "For concentrated power and profound comprehension of things only two other Greek writers can stand with Thucydides: one is Aeschylus, and the other is the poet who wrote the *Iliad*."

I thought he would be likely to express them, while at the same time I endeavored, as nearly as I could, to give the general purport of what was actually said. Of the events of the war I have not ventured to speak from any chance information, nor according to any notion of my own; I have described nothing but what I either saw myself, or learned from others of whom I made the most careful and particular inquiry. The task was a laborious one, because eye-witnesses of the same occurrences gave different accounts of them, as they remembered or were interested in the actions of one side or the other."[5] Thucydides believed in the importance of detailing the unfolding years of the war and though in the midst of them, writes ever dramatically, seriously, intently.

"The little that we know about Thucydides is furnished by himself," writes the classicist Edward Capps. "At the outbreak of the Peloponnesian war, in 431 B. C., he was a man of maturity; we may therefore place the date of his birth about 470 B. C. An Athenian by birth, his father's family were originally Thracians, closely related to the wife of Miltiades, the hero of Marathon. We can only conjecture what were the influences which surrounded his youth and early manhood; but since his family was wealthy and influential, and he himself exceptionally endowed by nature, we may believe that he participated fully in the marvelous and many-sided culture for which the age of Pericles was distinguished. For a time after the outbreak of the war he was one of the Athenian generals. In 424 B. C. an event occurred, however, which doubt-less seemed a heavy misfortune to him, though in reality it was the turning-point of his life and opened to him the career for which his talents best fitted him. While he was in command of an Athenian fleet off the Thracian coast, the Spartan general Brasidas surprised and captured Amphipolis, the principal Athenian possession in northern Greece. Thucydides was near enough to have prevented the capture of the stronghold, but he lingered in the neighborhood of some gold mines which belonged to him and arrived too late. Whatever the reason was for his delay, the Athenians promptly deprived him of his command, and he lived in exile for twenty years, until the end of the war in 404 B. C. During this time he followed the war closely, gathered facts from the Spartan as well as

---

[5] *Thucydides Translated into English, With Introduction, Marginal Analysis, Notes, and Indices.* Translated by Benjamin Jowett. Oxford at the Clarendon Press. 1881. I: 22.

from the Athenian side, visited many important sites, probably including Sicily, and thus laboriously and conscientiously got together the materials for his history. He died about 398 B. C."[6]

The speeches Thucydides relates are always closely reasoned; *everybody* in his history is similar in that they're *smart*, even the "most violent" of Athenians Cleon, who, in the midst of ruthless and cynical insights, occasionally startles us with simple brilliance: "Mankind apparently find it easier to drive away adversity than to retain prosperity." Thucydides does not admire chameleons like Alcibiades, but he presents in quick, sharp strokes Alcibiades' energy, talents and peculiarities: "He had a great position among the citizens and was devoted to horseracing and other pleasures which outran his means. And in the end his wild courses went far to ruin the Athenian state." The objection that Thucydides was not an eyewitness to *all* of the speeches and his own admission that the speeches are at least in part creations of his understanding of the men and events he narrates does not diminish or distract from the speeches' power and illumination. History's great speeches have rarely been, until fairly recently when electronic recordings have been possible, actual transcriptions. We have vast evidence, for instance, of discrepant reportage of speeches during the American Civil War and even today, we note the discrepancies between press releases of political speeches and their actual deliveries.

There's no going back 2,500 years, so we're left with the gold Thucydides, among others, mined for us. Quintilian observes, "Do we have access to these outstanding speakers in any way other than through their writings?" We have Plato's extraordinary rendering of Socrates' defense during his trial in 399 B.C. and, just as fortunate, we have the make-shift general Xenophon's account of the speech he himself delivered to the survivors of the Greek mercenary army that had to fight their way out of Asia Minor. (Apparently, speechmakers did not write down or publish their own words until the fourth century B.C.) We meet Demosthenes in two speeches he set down in print, though the classicist Catherine Steel cautions us that "written versions of speeches are rather peculiar things which occupy an inescapably secondary position, deriving much of their meaning from an event of which they are now

---

[6]Edward Capps. *From Homer to Theocritus: A Manual of Greek Literature*. New York: Charles Scribner's Sons. 1901.

the only, partial, record."[7] True enough, but with these speakers, "partial" is still awfully good.

The Roman historians Sallust and Livy and Tacitus, something in the manner of Thucydides, offer speeches for the heroes of Roman history that are dramatic and inspiring. The most prominent orator of Rome, Cicero, was famous for his speeches even when he did not apparently always deliver the speech himself (as in his Second Philippic). Cicero, unlike the Greeks, asserted his personality the way a character actor might, and flavors the tone with his distinctive personality throughout.

So while these exciting speeches are certainly not transcripts, we believe in them the way readers have forever believed in the truth of storytelling about real events. We weigh them and are captivated by the vigor and the expressiveness of their words: "When a man insists that words ought not to be our guides in action," argues the Athenian Diodotus (a debater known to us only because of Thucydides), "he is either wanting in sense or wanting in honesty: he is wanting in sense if he does not see that there is no other way in which we can throw light on the unknown future . . ."[8]

In my selections I have relied first on my love of Thucydides and next on the knowledge and work of editors of previous collections of oratory, most notably Guy Carleton Lee. The speeches by the "Attic Orators" are scarcely represented, because most of their extant speeches are legal arguments or cases; the speeches from history seem more dramatic and more compelling, less clever and calculated, more spontaneous and of greater impact. Demosthenes, the most admired of Greek orators, has many speeches that seem to me legal exercises, models of persuasiveness and construction—yet less vital than the speeches in which he is mesmerizing not a courtroom jury but an assembly of citizens or soldiers.

Occasionally I quote from the historians' narratives to provide some of the immediate dramatic context of the speeches and to link one speech's response to the next. I have not cut or abridged the speeches from the sources, but it's worth reminding ourselves that the history behind each speech is rich and deep—and available in some of the most spellbinding historical works ever written,

---

[7]Catherine Steel. *Roman Oratory*. Cambridge: Cambridge University Press for the Classical Association. 2006. 26.
[8]See below, page 39.

some of which I have listed in the bibliography. I have used American spelling throughout and added paragraph breaks; though some of the translations are centuries old, only a handful of rephrasings seemed to be needed. English translators have always well appreciated the vigor and directness of the Greeks and Romans.

ARCHIDAMUS and STHENELAIDAS

RESPONSES TO THE ADDRESSES OF THE CORINTHIANS AND THE ATHENIANS ON SPARTA GOING TO WAR AGAINST ATHENS
(432 B.C.)

This selection, a series of four speeches, at the Peloponnesian Confederacy's Congress at Sparta, comes from Part 1 of Thucydides' *History of the Peloponnesian War.* The war, between Sparta (situated on the Peloponnese) and its allies and Athens and its allies, lasted twenty-seven years, from 431 until 404 B.C., and resulted in the defeat of Athenian cultural and political dominance in Greece. The first of the speeches, by the Corinthians, is an attempt to goad the Lacedaemonians (Spartans) into war by reminding them of the encroachments of Athens, most recently into Potidea.

Famously and extraordinarily, the Corinthians sum up the character of the Athenians in a way that continues to resound—and which the Athenians themselves would not have resented: "They are revolutionary, equally quick in the conception and in the execution of every new plan . . . They are bold beyond their strength; they run risks which prudence would condemn; and in the midst of misfortune they are full of hope. . . . They are impetuous . . . For they hope to gain something by leaving their homes . . . When conquerors, they pursue their victory to the utmost; when defeated, they fall back the least. Their bodies they devote to their country as though they belonged to other men; their true self is their mind, which is most truly their own when employed in her service.

1

When they do not carry out an intention which they have formed, they seem to themselves to have sustained a personal bereavement; when an enterprise succeeds, they have gained a mere installment of what is to come; but if they fail, they at once conceive new hopes and so fill up the void. With them alone to hope is to have, for they lose not a moment in the execution of an idea. This is the lifelong task, full of danger and toil, which they are always imposing upon themselves. None enjoy their good things less, because they are always seeking for more. To do their duty is their only holiday, and they deem the quiet of inaction to be as disagreeable as the most tiresome business. If a man should say of them, in a word, that they were born neither to have peace themselves, nor to allow peace to other men, he would simply speak the truth."[1]

The Athenian embassy then makes the case for continued peace: "How moderate we are would speedily appear if others took our place; indeed our very moderation, which should be our glory, has been unjustly converted into a reproach." Then, with the Corinthians and Athenians cleared out of the meeting and addressing only the Spartans themselves, King Archidamus cautions his people about the realities of war: "We must not for one moment flatter ourselves that if we do but ravage their country the war will be at an end. Nay, I fear that we shall bequeath it to our children; for the Athenians with their high spirit will never barter their liberty to save their land, or be terrified like novices at the sight of war. . . . For if we allow ourselves to be stung into premature action by the reproaches of our allies, and waste their country before we are ready, we shall only involve Peloponnesus in more and more difficulty and disgrace." Last of all, briefly but intelligently, is the Spartan ephor (judge) Sthenelaidas, who forces an immediate vote on the war in the assembly.

[Thucydides' narrative:] *The Aeginetans did not venture to send envoys openly, but secretly they acted with the Corinthians, and were among the*

---

[1]The American classicist Bernard Knox remarks of this passage: "Thucydides gives us a remarkable estimate by Athens' enemies, the Corinthians, of the heroic, almost demonic, militancy deployed by the city that had, by its invention of democracy, liberated the creative energies of its own population and saved Greece." *Backing into the Future: The Classical Tradition and Its Renewal.* New York: W. W. Norton and Company. 1994. 141.

chief instigators of the war, declaring that they had been robbed of the independence which the treaty guaranteed them. The Lacedaemonians themselves then proceeded to summon any of the allies who had similar charges to bring against the Athenians, and calling their own ordinary assembly told them to speak. Several of them came forward and stated their wrongs. The Megarians alleged, among other grounds of complaint, that they were excluded from all harbors within the Athenian dominion and from the Athenian market, contrary to the treaty. The Corinthians waited until the other allies had stirred up the Lacedaemonians; at length they came forward, and, last of all, spoke as follows:

[The Corinthian representatives]

The spirit of trust, Lacedaemonians, which animates your own political and social life, makes you distrust others who, like ourselves, have something unpleasant to say, and this temper of mind, though favorable to moderation, too often leaves you in ignorance of what is going on outside your own country. Time after time we have warned you of the mischief which the Athenians would do to us, but instead of taking our words to heart, you chose to suspect that we only spoke from interested motives. And this is the reason why you have brought the allies to Sparta too late, not before but after the injury has been inflicted, and when they are smarting under the sense of it. Which of them all has a better right to speak than ourselves, who have the heaviest accusations to make, outraged as we are by the Athenians, and neglected by you? If the crimes which they are committing against Hellas were being done in a corner, then you might be ignorant, and we should have to inform you of them: but now, what need of many words? Some of us, as you see, have been already enslaved; they are at this moment intriguing against others, notably against allies of ours; and long ago they had made all their preparations in the prospect of war. Else why did they seduce from her allegiance Corcyra, which they still hold in defiance of us, and why are they blockading Potidaea, the latter a most advantageous post for the command of the Thracian peninsula, the former a great naval power which might have assisted the Peloponnesians?

And the blame of all this rests on you; for you originally allowed them to fortify their city after the Persian War, and afterwards to build their Long Walls; and to this hour you have gone on

defrauding of liberty their unfortunate subjects, and are now beginning to take it away from your own allies. For the true enslaver of
a people is he who can put an end to their slavery but has no care
about it; and all the more, if he be reputed the champion of liberty
in Hellas. And so we have met at last, but with what difficulty! And
even now we have no definite object. By this time we ought to
have been considering, not whether we are wronged, but how we
are to be revenged. The aggressor is not now threatening, but
advancing; he has made up his mind, while we are resolved about
nothing. And we know too well how by slow degrees and with
stealthy steps the Athenians encroach upon their neighbors. While
they think that you are too dull to observe them, they are more
careful, but when they know that you willfully overlook their
aggressions, they will strike and not spare.

Of all Hellenes, Lacedaemonians, you are the only people who
never do anything: on the approach of an enemy you are content
to defend yourselves against him, not by acts, but by intentions, and
seek to overthrow him, not in the infancy but in the fullness of his
strength. How came you to be considered safe? That reputation of
yours was never justified by facts. We all know that the Persian
made his way from the ends of the earth against Peloponnesus
before you encountered him in a worthy manner; and now you are
blind to the doings of the Athenians, who are not at a distance as
he was, but close at hand. Instead of attacking your enemy, you
wait to be attacked, and take the chances of a struggle which has
been deferred until his power is doubled. And you know that the
Barbarian miscarried chiefly through his own errors; and that we
have oftener been delivered from these very Athenians by blunders
of their own, than by any aid from you. Some have already been
ruined by the hopes which you inspired in them; for so entirely did
they trust you that they took no precautions themselves. These
things we say in no accusing or hostile spirit—let that be under-
stood—but by way of expostulation. For men expostulate with
erring friends; they bring accusation against enemies who have
done them a wrong.

And surely we have a right to find fault with our neighbors, if
anyone ever had. There are important interests at stake to which,
as far as we can see, you are insensible. And you have never considered what manner of men are these Athenians with whom you
will have to fight, and how utterly unlike yourselves. They are

revolutionary, equally quick in the conception and in the execution of every new plan; while you are conservative—careful only to keep what you have, originating nothing, and not acting even when action is most urgent. They are bold beyond their strength; they run risks which prudence would condemn; and in the midst of misfortune they are full of hope. Whereas it is your nature, though strong, to act feebly; when your plans are most prudent, to distrust them; and when calamities come upon you, to think that you will never be delivered from them. They are impetuous, and you are dilatory; they are always abroad, and you are always at home. For they hope to gain something by leaving their homes; but you are afraid that any new enterprise may imperil what you have already. When conquerors, they pursue their victory to the utmost; when defeated, they fall back the least. Their bodies they devote to their country as though they belonged to other men; their true self is their mind, which is most truly their own when employed in her service. When they do not carry out an intention which they have formed, they seem to themselves to have sustained a personal bereavement; when an enterprise succeeds, they have gained a mere installment of what is to come; but if they fail, they at once conceive new hopes and so fill up the void. With them alone to hope is to have, for they lose not a moment in the execution of an idea. This is the lifelong task, full of danger and toil, which they are always imposing upon themselves. None enjoy their good things less, because they are always seeking for more. To do their duty is their only holiday, and they deem the quiet of inaction to be as disagreeable as the most tiresome business. If a man should say of them, in a word, that they were born neither to have peace themselves, nor to allow peace to other men, he would simply speak the truth.

In the face of such an enemy, Lacedaemonians, you persist in doing nothing. You do not see that peace is best secured by those who use their strength justly, but whose attitude shows that they have no intention of submitting to wrong. Justice with you seems to consist in giving no annoyance to others and in defending yourselves only against positive injury. But this policy would hardly be successful, even if your neighbors were like yourselves; and in the present case, as we pointed out just now, your ways compared with theirs are old-fashioned. And, as in the arts, so also in politics, the new must always prevail over the old. In settled times the

traditions of government should be observed: but when circumstances are changing and men are compelled to meet them, much
originality is required. The Athenians have had a wider experience, and therefore the administration of their state unlike yours
has been greatly reformed. But here let your procrastination end;
send an army at once into Attica and assist your allies, especially
the Potidaeans, to whom your word is pledged. Do not betray
friends and kindred into the hands of their worst enemies; or drive
us in despair to seek the alliance of others; in taking such a course
we should be doing nothing wrong either before the gods who are
the witnesses of our oaths, or before men whose eyes are upon us.
For the true breakers of treaties are not those who, when forsaken,
turn to others, but those who forsake allies whom they have sworn
to defend. We will remain your friends if you choose to bestir
yourselves; for we should be guilty of an impiety if we deserted
you without cause; and we shall not easily find allies equally con-
genial to us. Take heed then: you have inherited from your fathers
the leadership of Peloponnesus; see that her greatness suffers no
diminution at your hands.

[Thucydides' narrative:] *Thus spoke the Corinthians. Now there happened to be staying at Lacedaemon an Athenian embassy which had come
on other business, and when the envoys heard what the Corinthians had
said, they felt bound to go before the Lacedaemonian assembly, not with the
view of answering the accusations brought against them by the cities, but
they wanted to put the whole question before the Lacedaemonians, and
make them understand that they should take time to deliberate and not be
rash. They also desired to set forth the greatness of their city, reminding the
elder men of what they knew, and informing the younger of what lay
beyond their experience. They thought that their words would sway the
Lacedaemonians in the direction of peace. So they came and said that, if
they might be allowed, they too would like to address the people. The
Lacedaemonians invited them to come forward, and they spoke as follows:*

[The Athenian representatives]

We were not sent here to argue with your allies, but on a special
mission; observing, however, that no small outcry has arisen against
us, we have come forward, not to answer the accusations which
they bring (for you are not judges before whom either we or they

have to plead), but to prevent you from lending too ready an ear to their bad advice and so deciding wrongly about a very serious question. We propose also, in reply to the wider charges which are raised against us, to show that what we have acquired we hold rightfully and that our city is not to be despised.

Of the ancient deeds handed down by tradition and which no eye of anyone who hears us ever saw, why should we speak? But of the Persian War, and other events which you yourselves remember, speak we must, although we have brought them forward so often that the repetition of them is disagreeable to us. When we faced those perils we did so for the common benefit: in the solid good you shared, and of the glory, whatever good there may be in that, we would not be wholly deprived. Our words are not designed to deprecate hostility, but to set forth in evidence the character of the city with which, unless you are very careful, you will soon be involved in war. We tell you that we, first and alone, dared to engage with the Barbarian at Marathon, and that when he came again, being too weak to defend ourselves by land, we and our whole people embarked on shipboard and shared with the other Hellenes in the victory of Salamis. Thereby he was prevented from sailing to the Peloponnesus and ravaging city after city; for against so mighty a fleet how could you have helped one another? He himself is the best witness of our words; for when he was once defeated at sea, he felt that his power was gone and quickly retreated with the greater part of his army.

The event proved undeniably that the fate of Hellas depended on her navy. And the three chief elements of success were contributed by us; namely, the greatest number of ships, the ablest general, the most devoted patriotism. The ships in all numbered four hundred, and of these, our own contingent amounted to nearly two-thirds. To the influence of Themistocles our general it was chiefly due that we fought in the strait, which was confessedly our salvation; and for this service you yourselves honored him above any stranger who ever visited you. Thirdly, we displayed the most extraordinary courage and devotion; there was no one to help us by land; for up to our frontier those who lay in the enemy's path were already slaves; so we determined to leave our city and sacrifice our homes. Even in that extremity we did not choose to desert the cause of the allies who still resisted, or by dispersing ourselves to become useless to them; but we embarked and fought, taking

no offence at your failure to assist us sooner. We maintain then that
we rendered you a service at least as great as you rendered us. The
cities from which you came to help us were still inhabited and you
might hope to return to them; your concern was for yourselves and
not for us; at any rate you remained at a distance while we had
anything to lose. But we went forth from a city which was no
more, and fought for one of which there was small hope; and yet
we saved ourselves, and bore our part in saving you. If, in order to
preserve our land, like other states, we had gone over to the
Persians at first, or afterwards had not ventured to embark because
our ruin was already complete, it would have been useless for you
with your weak navy to fight at sea, but everything would have
gone quietly just as the Persian desired.

Considering, Lacedaemonians, the energy and sagacity which we
then displayed, do we deserve to be so bitterly hated by the other
Hellenes merely because we have an empire? That empire was not
acquired by force; but you would not stay and make an end of the
Barbarian, and the allies came of their own accord and asked us to
be their leaders. The subsequent development of our power was
originally forced upon us by circumstances; fear was our first
motive; afterwards honor, and then interest stepped in. And when
we had incurred the hatred of most of our allies; when some of
them had already revolted and been subjugated, and you were no
longer the friends to us which you once had been, but suspicious
and ill-disposed, how could we without great risk relax our hold?
For the cities as fast as they fell away from us would have gone over
to you. And no man is to be reproached who seizes every possible
advantage when the danger is so great.

At all events, Lacedaemonians, we may retort that you, in the
exercise of your supremacy, manage the cities of Peloponnesus to
suit your own views; and that if you, and not we, had persevered
in the command of the allies long enough to be hated, you would
have been quite as intolerable to them as we are, and would have
been compelled, for the sake of your own safety, to rule with a
strong hand. An empire was offered to us: can you wonder that,
acting as human nature always will, we accepted it and refused to
give it up again, constrained by three all-powerful motives, honor,
fear, interest? We are not the first who have aspired to rule; the
world has ever held that the weaker must be kept down by the
stronger. And we think that we are worthy of power; and there was

a time when you thought so too; but now, when you mean expediency you talk about justice. Did justice ever deter anyone from taking by force whatever he could? Men who indulge the natural ambition of empire deserve credit if they are in any degree more careful of justice than they need be. How moderate we are would speedily appear if others took our place; indeed our very moderation, which should be our glory, has been unjustly converted into a reproach.

For because in our suits with our allies, regulated by treaty, we do not even stand upon our rights, but have instituted the practice of deciding them at Athens and by Athenian law, we are supposed to be litigious. None of our opponents observe why others, who exercise dominion elsewhere and are less moderate than we are in their dealings with their subjects, escape this reproach. Why is it? Because men who practice violence have no longer any need of law. But we are in the habit of meeting our allies on terms of equality, and, therefore, if through some legal decision of ours, or exercise of our imperial power, contrary to their own ideas of right, they suffer ever so little, they are not grateful for our moderation in leaving them so much, but are far more offended at their trifling loss than if we had from the first plundered them in the face of day, laying aside all thought of law. For then they would themselves have admitted that the weaker must give way to the stronger. Mankind resent injustice more than violence, because the one seems to be an unfair advantage taken by an equal, the other is the irresistible force of a superior. They were patient under the yoke of the Persian who inflicted on them far more grievous wrongs; but now our dominion is odious in their eyes. And no wonder: the ruler of the day is always detested by his subjects. And should your empire supplant ours, may not you lose the good-will which you owe to the fear of us? Lose it you certainly will, if you mean again to exhibit the temper of which you gave a specimen when, for a short time, you led the confederacy against the Persian. For the institutions under which you live are incompatible with those of foreign states; and further, when any of you goes abroad, he respects neither these nor any other Hellenic customs.

Do not then be hasty in deciding a question which is serious; and do not, by listening to representations and complaints which concern others, bring trouble upon yourselves. Realize, while there is time, the inscrutable nature of war; and how when protracted it generally ends in becoming a mere matter of chance, over which neither of us can have any control, the event being equally unknown and equally hazardous to both. The misfortune is that in their hurry to go to war, men begin with blows, and when a reverse comes upon them, then have recourse to words. But neither you nor we have as yet committed this mistake; and therefore, while both of us can still choose the prudent part, we tell you not to break the peace or violate your oaths. Let our differences be determined by arbitration, according to the treaty. If you refuse we call to witness the gods, by whom your oaths were sworn, that you are the authors of the war; and we will do our best to strike in return.

[Thucydides' narrative:] *When the Lacedaemonians had heard the charges brought by the allies against the Athenians, and their rejoinder, they ordered everybody but themselves to withdraw, and deliberated alone. The majority were agreed that there was now a clear case against the Athenians, and that they must fight at once. But Archidamus their king, who was held to be both an able and a prudent man, came forward and spoke as follows:*

[Archidamus]

At my age, Lacedaemonians, I have had experience of many wars, and I see several of you who are as old as I am, and who will not, as men too often do, desire war because they have never known it, or in the belief that it is either a good or a safe thing. Anyone who calmly reflects will find that the war about which you are now deliberating is likely to be a very great one. When we encounter our neighbors in the Peloponnese, their mode of fighting is like ours, and they are all within a short march. But when we have to do with men whose country is a long way off, and who are most skilful seamen and thoroughly provided with the means of war,— having wealth, private and public, ships, horses, infantry, and a population larger than is to be found in any single Hellenic terri- tory, not to speak of the numerous allies who pay them tribute,—is this a people against whom we can lightly take up arms or plunge into a contest unprepared? To what do we trust? To our navy? There we are inferior; and to exercise and train ourselves until we are a match for them will take time. To our money? Nay, but in that we are weaker still; we have none in a common treasury, and we are never willing to contribute out of our private means.

Perhaps someone may be encouraged by the superior equipment and numbers of our infantry, which will enable us regularly to invade and ravage their lands. But their empire extends to distant countries, and they will be able to introduce supplies by sea. Or, again, we may try to stir up revolts among their allies. But these are mostly islanders, and we shall have to employ a fleet in their defense, as well as in our own. How then shall we carry on the war? For if we can neither defeat them at sea, nor deprive them of the revenues by which their navy is maintained, we shall get the worst of it. And having gone so far, we shall no longer be able even to make peace with honor, especially if we are believed to have begun the quarrel. We must not for one moment flatter ourselves that if we do but ravage their country the war will be at an end. Nay, I fear that we shall bequeath it to our children; for the Athenians with their high spirit will never barter their liberty to save their land, or be terrified like novices at the sight of war.

Not that I would have you shut your eyes to their designs and abstain from unmasking them, or tamely suffer them to injure our allies. But do not take up arms yet. Let us first send and remonstrate with them: we need not let them know positively whether we intend to go to war or not. In the meantime our own preparations may be going forward; we may seek for allies wherever we can find them, whether in Hellas or among the Barbarians, who will supply our deficiencies in ships and money. Those who, like ourselves, are exposed to Athenian intrigue cannot be blamed if in self-defense they seek the aid, not of Hellenes only, but of Barbarians. And we must develop our own resources to the utmost. If they listen to our ambassadors, well and good; but, if not, in two or three years' time we shall be in a stronger position, should we then determine to attack them. Perhaps too when they begin to see that we are getting ready, and that our words are to be interpreted by our actions, they may be more likely to yield; for their fields will be still untouched and their goods undespoiled, and it will be in their power to save them by their decision. Think of their land simply in the light of a hostage, all the more valuable in proportion as it is better cultivated; you should spare it as long as you can, and not by reducing them to despair make their resistance more obstinate. For if we allow ourselves to be stung into premature action by the reproaches of our allies, and waste their country before we are ready, we shall only involve Peloponnesus in more and more difficulty and disgrace.

Charges brought by cities or persons against one another can be satisfactorily arranged; but when a great confederacy, in order to satisfy private grudges, undertakes a war of which no man can foresee the issue, it is not easy to terminate it with honor. And let no one think that there is any want of courage in cities so numerous hesitating to attack a single one. The allies of the Athenians are not less numerous; they pay them tribute too; and war is not an affair of arms, but of money which gives to arms their use, and which is needed above all things when a continental is fighting against a maritime power: let us find money first, and then we may safely allow our minds to be excited by the speeches of our allies. We, on whom the future responsibility, whether for good or evil, will chiefly fall, should calmly reflect on the consequences which may follow.

Do not be ashamed of the slowness and procrastination with which they are so fond of charging you; if you begin the war in haste, you will end it at your leisure, because you took up arms without sufficient preparation. Remember that we have always been citizens of a free and most illustrious state, and that for us the policy which they condemn may well be the truest good sense and discretion. It is a policy which has saved us from growing insolent in prosperity or giving way under adversity, like other men. We are not stimulated by the allurements of flattery into dangerous courses of which we disapprove; nor are we goaded by offensive charges into compliance with any man's wishes. Our habits of discipline make us both brave and wise; brave, because the spirit of loyalty quickens the sense of honor, and the sense of honor inspires courage; wise, because we are not so highly educated that we have learned to despise the laws, and are too severely trained and of too loyal a spirit to disobey them. We have not acquired that useless over-intelligence which makes a man an excellent critic of an enemy's plans, but paralyses him in the moment of action. We think that the wits of our enemies are as good as our own, and that the element of fortune cannot be forecast in words. Let us assume that they have common prudence, and let our preparations be, not words, but deeds. Our hopes ought not to rest on the probability of their making mistakes, but on our own caution and foresight. We should remember that one man is much the same as another, and that he is best who is trained in the severest school.

These are principles which our fathers have handed down to us, and we maintain to our lasting benefit; we must not lose sight of them, and when many lives and much wealth, many cities and a great name are at stake, we must not be hasty, or make up our minds in a few short hours; we must take time. We can afford to wait, when others cannot, because we are strong. And now, send to the Athenians and remonstrate with them about Potidaea first, and also about the other wrongs of which your allies complain. They say that they are willing to have the matter tried; and against one who offers to submit to justice you must not proceed as against a criminal until his cause has been heard. In the meantime prepare for war. This decision will be the best for yourselves and the most formidable to your enemies.

[Thucydides' narrative:] *Thus spoke Archidamus. Last of all, Sthenelaidas, at that time one of the Ephors, came forward and addressed the Lacedaemonians as follows:*

[Sthenelaidas]

I do not know what the long speeches of the Athenians mean. They have been loud in their own praise, but they do not pretend to say that they are dealing honestly with our allies and with the Peloponnesus. If they behaved well in the Persian War and are now behaving badly to us they ought to be punished twice over, because they were once good men and have become bad. But we are the same now as we were then, and we shall not do our duty if we allow our allies to be ill-used, and put off helping them, for they cannot put off their troubles. Others may have money and ships and horses, but we have brave allies and we must not betray them to the Athenians. If they were suffering in word only, by words and legal processes their wrongs might be redressed; but now there is not a moment to be lost, and we must help them with all our might. Let no one tell us that we should take time to think when we are suffering injustice. Nay, we reply, those who mean to do injustice should take a long time to think. Wherefore, Lacedaemonians, prepare for war as the honor of Sparta demands.

Withstand the advancing power of Athens. Do not let us betray our allies, but, with the gods on our side, let us attack the evil-doer.

[Thucydides' narrative:] *When Sthenelaidas had thus spoken he, being Ephor, himself put the question to the Lacedaemonian assembly. Their custom is to signify their decision by cries and not by voting. But he professed himself unable to tell on which side was the louder cry, and wishing to call forth a demonstration which might encourage the warlike spirit, he said, "Whoever of you, Lacedaemonians, thinks that the treaty has been broken and that the Athenians are in the wrong, let him rise and go yonder" (pointing to a particular spot), "and those who think otherwise to the other side."*

So the assembly rose and divided, and it was determined by a large majority that the treaty had been broken. The Lacedaemonians then recalled the allies and told them that in their judgment the Athenians were guilty, but that they wished to hold a general assembly of the allies and take a vote from them all; then the war, if they approved of it, might be undertaken by common consent. Having accomplished their purpose, the allies returned home; and the Athenian envoys, when their errand was done, returned likewise. Thirteen years of the thirty years' peace which was concluded after the recovery of Euboea had elapsed and the fourteenth year had begun when the Lacedaemonian assembly decided that the treaty had been broken.

In arriving at this decision and resolving to go to war, the Lacedaemonians were influenced, not so much by the speeches of their allies, as by the fear of the Athenians and of their increasing power. For they saw the greater part of Hellas already subject to them.

SOURCE: Benjamin Jowett. *Thucydides Translated into English, With Introduction, Marginal Analysis, Notes, and Indices.* Oxford at the Clarendon Press. 1881.

PERICLES

IN FAVOR OF THE WAR (432 B.C.)

Among the highlights of Thucydides' history is his presentation of the character and speeches of the Athenian hero Pericles (495–429 B.C.), whose fame and glory are completely imaginable to us *only* because of Thucydides' details. In the Athenian assembly, Pericles discusses the question of war against Sparta and comes to the conclusion that this war is necessary, even if it means the Athenians may have to leave their city: "Mourn not for houses and lands, but for men; men may gain these, but these will not gain men."

[Thucydides' narrative:] *Many came forward to speak, and much was said on both sides, some affirming that they ought to go to war, and others that this decree about the Megarians should be rescinded and not stand in the way of peace. At last Pericles, the son of Xanthippus, who was the first man of his day at Athens, and the greatest orator and statesman, came forward and advised as follows:*

Athenians, I say, as I always have said, that we must never yield to the Peloponnesians, although I know that men are persuaded to go to war in one temper of mind, and act when the time comes in another, and that their resolutions change with the changes of fortune. But I see that I must give you the same or nearly the same advice which I gave before, and I call upon those whom my words may convince to maintain our united determination, even if we should not escape disaster; or else, if our sagacity be justified by success, to claim no share of the credit. The movement of events is

15

often wayward and incomprehensible as the course of human thought; and this is why we ascribe to chance whatever belies our calculation.

For some time past the designs of the Lacedaemonians have been clear enough, and they are still clearer now. Our agreement says that when differences arise, the two parties shall refer them to arbitration, and in the meantime both are to retain what they have. But for arbitration they never ask; and when it is offered by us, they refuse it. They want to redress their grievances by arms and not by argument; and now they come to us, using the language, no longer of expostulation, but of command. They tell us to quit Potidaea, to leave Aegina independent, and to rescind the decree respecting the Megarians. These last ambassadors go further still, and announce that we must give the Hellenes independence. I would have none of you imagine that we will be fighting for a small matter if we refuse to annul the Megarian decree, of which they make so much, telling us that its revocation would prevent the war. You should have no lingering uneasiness about this; you are not really going to war for a trifle. For in the seeming trifle is involved the trial and confirmation of your whole purpose. If you yield to them in a small matter, they will think that you are afraid, and will immediately dictate some more oppressive condition; but if you are firm, you will prove to them that they must treat you as their equals.

Wherefore make up your minds once for all, either to give way while you are still unharmed, or, if we are going to war, as in my judgment is best, then on no plea small or great to give way at all; we will not condescend to possess our own in fear. Any claim, the smallest as well as the greatest, imposed on a neighborhood and an equal when there has been no legal award, can mean nothing but slavery.

That our resources are equal to theirs, and that we shall be as strong in the war, I will now prove to you in detail. The Peloponnesians cultivate their own lands, and they have no wealth either public or private. Nor have they any experience of long wars in countries beyond the sea; their poverty prevents them from fighting, except in person against each other, and that for a short time only. Such men cannot be often manning fleets or sending out armies. They would be at a distance from their own properties, upon which they must nevertheless draw, and they will be kept off the sea by us. Now wars are supported out of accumulated wealth, and not out of forced contributions. And men who cultivate their own lands are more ready to serve with their persons than with their property; they do not despair of their lives, but they soon grow anxious lest their money should all be spent, especially if the war in which they are engaged is protracted beyond their calculation, as may well be the case.

In a single pitched battle the Peloponnesians and their allies are a match for all Hellas, but they are not able to maintain a war against a power different in kind from their own; they have no regular general assembly, and therefore cannot execute their plans with speed and decision. The confederacy is made up of many races; all the representatives have equal votes, and press their several interests. There follows the usual result, that nothing is ever done properly. For some are all anxiety to be revenged on an enemy, while others only want to get off with as little loss as possible. The members of such a confederacy are slow to meet, and when they do meet, they give little time to the consideration of any common interest, and a great deal to schemes which further the interest of their particular state. Everyone fancies that his own neglect will do no harm, but that it is somebody else's business to keep a look-out for him, and this idea, cherished alike by each, is the secret ruin of all.

Their greatest difficulty will be want of money, which they can only provide slowly; delay will thus occur, and war waits for no man. Further, no fortified place which they can raise against us is to be feared any more than their navy. As to the first, even in time of peace it would be hard for them to build a city able to compete with Athens; and how much more so when they are in an enemy's country, and our walls will be a menace to them quite as much as theirs to us! Or, again, if they simply raise a fort in our territory, they may do mischief to some part of our lands by sallies, and the slaves may desert to them; but that will not prevent us from sailing to the Peloponnese and there raising forts against them, and defending ourselves there by the help of our navy, which is our strong arm. For we have gained more experience of fighting on land from warfare at sea than they of naval affairs from warfare on land. And they will not easily acquire the art of seamanship; even you yourselves, who have been practicing ever since the Persian War, are not yet perfect. How can they, who are not sailors, but tillers of the soil, do much? They will not even be permitted to practice, because a large fleet will constantly be lying in wait for them. If they were watched by a few ships only, they might run the risk, trusting to their numbers and forgetting their inexperience; but if they are kept off the sea by our superior strength, their want of practice will make them unskillful, and their want of skill timid. Maritime skill is like skill of other kinds, not a thing to be cultivated by the way or at chance times; it is jealous of any other pursuit which distracts the mind for an instant from itself.

Suppose, again, that they lay hands on the treasures at Olympia and Delphi, and tempt our mercenary sailors with the offer of higher pay, there might be serious danger, if we and our metics[1] embarking alone were not still a match for them. But we are a match for them; and, best of all, our pilots are taken from our own citizens, while no sailors are to be found so good or so numerous as ours in all the rest of Hellas. None of our mercenaries will choose to fight on their side for the sake of a few days' high pay, when he will not only be an exile, but will incur greater danger, and will have less hope of victory.

Such I conceive to be the prospects of the Peloponnesians. But we ourselves are free from the defects which I have noted in them; and we have great advantages. If they attack our country by land, we shall attack theirs by sea; and the devastation, even of part of Peloponnesus, will be a very different thing from that of all Attica. For they, if they want fresh territory, must take it by arms, whereas we have abundance of land both in the islands and on the continent; such is the power which the empire of the sea gives. Reflect, if we were islanders, who would be more invulnerable? Let us imagine that we are, and acting in that spirit let us give up land and houses, but keep a watch over the city and the sea. We should not under any irritation at the loss of our property give battle to the Peloponnesians, who far outnumber us. If we conquer, we shall have to fight over again with as many more; and if we fail, besides the defeat, our confederacy, which is our strength, will be lost to us; for our allies will rise in revolt when we are no longer capable of making war upon them. Mourn not for houses and lands, but for men; men may gain these, but these will not gain men. If I thought that you would listen to me, I would say to you, "Go yourselves

---

[1]*metics*: resident-aliens

and destroy them, and thereby prove to the Peloponnesians that none of these things will move you."

I have many other reasons for believing that you will conquer, but you must not be extending your empire while you are at war, or run into unnecessary dangers. I am more afraid of our own mistakes than of our enemies' designs. But of all this I will speak again when the time of action comes; for the present, let us send the ambassadors away, giving them this answer: "That we will not exclude the Megarians from our markets and harbors, if the Lacedaemonians will cease to expel foreigners, whether ourselves or our allies, from Sparta; for the treaty no more forbids the one than the other. That we will concede independence to the cities, if they were independent when we made the treaty no more forbids the one than the other, their allied states a true independence, not for the interest of Lacedaemon, but everywhere for their own. Also that we are willing to offer arbitration according to the treaty. And that we do not want to begin a war, but intend to defend ourselves if attacked." This answer will be just, and befits the dignity of the city. We must be aware however that war will come; and the more willing we are to accept the situation, the less ready will our enemies be to lay hands upon us.

Remember that where dangers are greatest, there the greatest honors are to be won by men and states. Our fathers, when they withstood the Persian, had no such power as we have; what little they had they forsook: not by good fortune but by wisdom, and not by power but by courage, they drove the Barbarian away and raised us to our present height of greatness. We must be worthy of them, and resist our enemies to the utmost, that we may hand down our empire unimpaired to posterity.

[Thucydides' narrative:] *Such were the words of Pericles. The Athenians, approving, voted as he told them, and on his motion answered the Lacedaemonians in detail as he had suggested, and on the whole question to the effect "that they would do nothing upon compulsion, but were ready to settle their differences by arbitration upon fair terms according to the treaty." So the ambassadors went home and came no more.*

SOURCE: Benjamin Jowett. *Thucydides Translated into English, With Introduction, Marginal Analysis, Notes, and Indices.* Oxford at the Clarendon Press. 1881.

PERICLES

FUNERAL SPEECH (431/430 B.C.)

The most famous of Pericles' speeches is, besides a testimonial to the greatness of Athens, a eulogy for "the men killed in the first year of the war that, beginning in 431 B.C., was to last twenty-seven years and in the end strip Athens of its fleet, its empire, and for a few months even its democracy," writes the classicist Bernard Knox. "When Pericles delivered this speech he could not know and could hardly imagine that the war would last so long and end that way, still less that he himself would in two years die of the plague that took such a toll of Athenian lives."[1]

[Thucydides' narrative:] *During the same winter, in accordance with an old national custom, the funeral of those who first fell in this war was celebrated by the Athenians at the public charge. The ceremony is as follows: Three days before the celebration they erect a tent in which the bones of the dead are laid out, and everyone brings to his own dead any offering which he pleases. At the time of the funeral the bones are placed in chests of cypress wood, which are conveyed on hearses; there is one chest for each tribe. They also carry a single empty litter decked with a pall for all whose bodies are missing, and cannot be recovered after the battle. The procession is accompanied by anyone who chooses, whether citizen or stranger, and the female relatives of the deceased are present at the place of interment and make lamentation. The public sepulcher is situated in the most beautiful spot*

---

[1]Bernard Knox. *Backing into the Future: The Classical Tradition and Its Renewal*. New York: W. W. Norton and Company. 1994. 146.

outside the walls; there they always bury those who fall in war; only after the battle of Marathon the dead, in recognition of their pre-eminent valor, were interred on the field. When the remains have been laid in the earth, some man of known ability and high reputation, chosen by the city, delivers a suitable oration over them; after which the people depart. Such is the manner of interment; and the ceremony was repeated from time to time throughout the war. Over those who were the first buried Pericles was chosen to speak. At the fitting moment he advanced from the sepulcher to a lofty stage, which had been erected in order that he might be heard as far as possible by the multitude, and spoke as follows:

Most of those who have spoken here before me have commended the law-giver who added this oration to our other funeral customs; it seemed to them a worthy thing that such an honor should be given at their burial to the dead who have fallen on the field of battle. But I should have preferred that, when men's deeds have been brave, they should be honored in deed only, and with such an honor as this public funeral, which you are now witnessing. Then the reputation of many would not have been imperiled on the eloquence or want of eloquence of one, and their virtues believed or not as he spoke well or ill. For it is difficult to say neither too little nor too much; and even moderation is apt not to give the impression of truthfulness. The friend of the dead who knows the facts is likely to think that the words of the speaker fall short of his knowledge and of his wishes; another who is not so well informed, when he hears of anything which surpasses his own powers, will be envious and will suspect exaggeration. Mankind are tolerant of the praises of others so long as each hearer thinks that he can do as well or nearly as well himself, but, when the speaker rises above him, jealousy is aroused and he begins to be incredulous. However, since our ancestors have set the seal of their approval upon the practice, I must obey, and to the utmost of my power shall endeavor to satisfy the wishes and beliefs of all who hear me.

I will speak first of our ancestors, for it is right and seemly that now, when we are lamenting the dead, a tribute should be paid to their memory. There has never been a time when they did not inhabit this land, which by their valor they have handed down from generation to generation, and we have received from them a free state. But if they were worthy of praise, still more were our fathers, who added to their inheritance, and after many a struggle transmitted to us their sons this great empire. And we ourselves assembled here today, who are still most of us in the vigor of life, have carried the work of improvement further, and have richly endowed our city with all things, so that she is sufficient for herself both in peace and war. Of the military exploits by which our various possessions were acquired, or of the energy with which we or our fathers drove back the tide of war, Hellenic or Barbarian, I will not speak; for the tale would be long and is familiar to you. But before I praise the dead, I should like to point out by what principles of action we rose to power, and under what institutions and through what manner of life our empire became great. For I conceive that such thoughts are not unsuited to the occasion, and that this numerous assembly of citizens and strangers may profitably listen to them.

Our form of government does not enter into rivalry with the institutions of others. We do not copy our neighbors, but are an example to them. It is true that we are called a democracy, for the administration is in the hands of the many and not of the few. But while the law secures equal justice to all alike in their private disputes, the claim of excellence is also recognized; and when a citizen is in any way distinguished, he is preferred to the public service, not as a matter of privilege, but as the reward of merit. Neither is poverty a bar, but a man may benefit his country whatever be the obscurity of his condition. There is no exclusiveness in our public life, and in our private intercourse we are not suspicious of one another, nor angry with our neighbor if he does what he likes; we do not put on sour looks at him which, though harmless, are not pleasant. While we are thus unconstrained in our private intercourse, a spirit of reverence pervades our public acts; we are prevented from doing wrong by respect for the authorities and for the laws, having an especial regard to those which are ordained for the protection of the injured as well as to those unwritten laws which bring upon the transgressor of them the reprobation of the general sentiment.

And we have not forgotten to provide for our weary spirits many relaxations from toil; we have regular games and sacrifices throughout the year; our homes are beautiful and elegant; and the delight which we daily feel in all these things helps to banish melancholy. Because of the greatness of our city the fruits of the whole earth flow in upon us; so that we enjoy the goods of other countries as freely as of our own.

Then, again, our military training is in many respects superior to that of our adversaries. Our city is thrown open to the world, and we never expel a foreigner or prevent him from seeing or learning anything of which the secret if revealed to an enemy might profit him. We rely not upon management or trickery, but upon our own hearts and hands. And in the matter of education, whereas they from early youth are always undergoing laborious exercises which are to make them brave, we live at ease, and yet are equally ready to face the perils which they face. And here is the proof. The Lacedaemonians come into Attica not by themselves, but with their whole confederacy following; we go alone into a neighbor's country; and although our opponents are fighting for their homes and we on a foreign soil, we have seldom any difficulty in overcoming them. Our enemies have never yet felt our united strength; the care of a navy divides our attention, and on land we are obliged to send our own citizens everywhere. But they, if they meet and defeat a part of our army, are as proud as if they had routed us all, and when defeated they pretend to have been vanquished by us all.

If then we prefer to meet danger with a light heart but without laborious training, and with a courage which is gained by habit and not enforced by law, are we not greatly the gainers? Since we do not anticipate the pain, although, when the hour comes, we can be as brave as those who never allow themselves to rest; and thus too our city is equally admirable in peace and in war. For we are lovers of the beautiful, yet simple in our tastes, and we cultivate the mind without loss of manliness. Wealth we employ, not for talk and ostentation, but when there is a real use for it. To avow poverty with us is no disgrace; the true disgrace is in doing nothing to avoid it. An Athenian citizen does not neglect the state because he takes care of his own household; and even those of us who are engaged in business have a very fair idea of politics. We alone regard a man who takes no interest in public affairs, not as a harmless, but as a useless character; and if few of us are originators, we are all sound judges of policy. The great impediment to action is, in our opinion, not discussion, but the want of that knowledge which is gained by discussion preparatory to action. For we have a peculiar power of thinking before we act and of acting too, whereas other men are courageous from ignorance but hesitate upon reflection. And they are surely to be esteemed the bravest spirits who, having the clearest sense both of the pains and pleasures of life, do not on that account shrink from danger. In doing good, again, we are unlike others; we make our friends by conferring, not by receiving favors. Now he who confers a favor is the firmer friend, because he would fain by kindness keep alive the memory of an obligation; but the recipient is colder in his feelings, because he knows that in requiting another's generosity he will not be winning gratitude but only paying a debt. We alone do good to our neighbors, not upon a calculation of interest, but in the confidence of freedom and in a frank and fearless spirit.

To sum up: I say that Athens is the school of Hellas, and that the individual Athenian in his own person seems to have the power of adapting himself to the most varied forms of action with the utmost versatility and grace. This is no passing and idle word, but truth and fact; and the assertion is verified by the position to which these qualities have raised the state. For in the hour of trial Athens alone among her contemporaries is superior to the report of her. No enemy who comes against her is indignant at the reverses which he sustains at the hands of such a city; no subject complains that his masters are unworthy of him. And we shall assuredly not be without witnesses; there are mighty monuments of our power which will make us the wonder of this and of succeeding ages; we shall not need the praises of Homer or of any other panegyrist whose poetry may please for the moment, although his representation of the facts will not bear the light of day. For we have compelled every land and every sea to open a path for our valor, and have everywhere planted eternal memorials of our friendship and of our enmity. Such is the city for whose sake these men nobly fought and died; they could not bear the thought that she might be taken from them; and every one of us who survive should gladly toil on her behalf.

I have dwelt upon the greatness of Athens because I want to show you that we are contending for a higher prize than those who enjoy none of these privileges, and to establish by manifest proof the merit of these men whom I am now commemorating. Their loftiest praise has been already spoken. For in magnifying the city I have magnified them, and men like them whose virtues made her glorious. And of how few Hellenes can it be said as of them, that their deeds when weighed in the balance have been found equal to their fame! Methinks that a death such as theirs has been gives the true measure of a man's worth; it may be the first revelation of his virtues, but is at any rate their final seal. For even those who come short in other ways may justly plead the valor with which they have fought for their country; they have blotted out the evil with the good, and have benefited the state more by their public services than they have injured her by their private actions. None of these men were enervated by wealth or hesitated to resign the pleasures of life; none of them put off the evil day in the hope, natural to poverty, that a man, though poor, may one day become rich. But, deeming that the punishment of their enemies was sweeter than any of these things, and that they could fall in no nobler cause, they determined at the hazard of their lives to be honorably avenged, and to leave the rest. They resigned to hope their unknown chance of happiness; but in the face of death they resolved to rely upon themselves alone. And when the moment came they were minded to resist and suffer, rather than to fly and save their lives; they ran away from the word of dishonor, but on the battlefield their feet stood fast, and in an instant, at the height of their fortune, they passed away from the scene, not of their fear, but of their glory.

Such was the end of these men; they were worthy of Athens, and the living need not desire to have a more heroic spirit, although they may pray for a less fatal issue. The value of such a spirit is not to be expressed in words. Anyone can discourse to you for ever about the advantages of a brave defense, which you know already. But instead of listening to him I would have you day by day fix your eyes upon the greatness of Athens, until you become filled with the love of her; and when you are impressed by the spectacle of her glory, reflect that this empire has been acquired by men who knew their duty and had the courage to do it, who in the hour of conflict had the fear of dishonor always present to them, and who, if ever they failed in an enterprise, would not allow their virtues to be lost to their country, but freely gave their lives to her as the fairest offering which they could present at her feast.

The sacrifice which they collectively made was individually repaid to them; for they received again each one for himself a praise which grows not old, and the noblest of all sepulchers—I speak not of that in which their remains are laid, but of that in which their glory survives, and is proclaimed always and on every fitting occasion both in word and deed. For the whole earth is the sepulcher of famous men; not only are they commemorated by columns and inscriptions in their own country, but in foreign lands there dwells also an unwritten memorial of them, graven not on stone but in the hearts of men. Make them your examples, and, esteeming courage to be freedom and freedom to be happiness, do not weigh too nicely the perils of war. The unfortunate who has no hope of a change for the better has less reason to throw away his life than the prosperous who, if he survive, is always liable to a change for the worse, and to whom any accidental fall makes the most serious difference. To a man of spirit, cowardice and disaster coming together are far more bitter than death striking him unperceived at a time when he is full of courage and animated by the general hope.

Wherefore I do not now commiserate the parents of the dead who stand here; I would rather comfort them. You know that your life has been passed amid manifold vicissitudes; and that they may be deemed fortunate who have gained most honor, whether an honorable death like theirs, or an honorable sorrow like yours, and whose days have been so ordered that the term of their happiness is likewise the term of their life. I know how hard it is to make you feel this, when the good fortune of others will too often remind you of the gladness which once lightened your hearts. And sorrow is felt at the want of those blessings, not which a man never knew, but which were a part of his life before they were taken from him. Some of you are of an age at which they may hope to have other children, and they ought to bear their sorrow better; not only will the children who may hereafter be born make them forget their own lost ones, but the city will be doubly a gainer. She will not be left desolate, and she will be safer. For a man's counsel cannot have equal weight or worth, when he alone has no children to risk in the general danger. To those of you who have passed their prime, I say: "Congratulate yourselves that you have been happy during the greater part of your days; remember that your life of sorrow will not last long, and be comforted by the glory of those who are gone. For the love of honor alone is ever young, and not riches, as some say, but honor is the delight of men when they are old and useless."

To you who are the sons and brothers of the departed, I see that the struggle to emulate them will be an arduous one. For all men praise the dead, and, however pre-eminent your virtue may be, hardly will you be thought, I do not say to equal, but even to approach them. The living have their rivals and detractors, but when a man is out of the way, the honor and good-will which he receives is unalloyed. And, if I am to speak of womanly virtues to those of you who will henceforth be widows, let me sum them up in one short admonition: To a woman not to show more weakness than is natural to her sex is a great glory, and not to be talked about for good or for evil among men.

I have paid the required tribute, in obedience to the law, making use of such fitting words as I had. The tribute of deeds has been paid in part; for the dead have been honorably interred, and it remains only that their children should be maintained at the public charge until they are grown up: this is the solid prize with which, as with a garland, Athens crowns her sons living and dead, after a struggle like theirs. For where the rewards of virtue are greatest, there the noblest citizens are enlisted in the service of the state. And now, when you have duly lamented, everyone his own dead, you may depart.

[Thucydides' narrative:] *Such was the order of the funeral celebrated in this winter, with the end of which ended the first year of the Peloponnesian War.*

SOURCE: Benjamin Jowett. *Thucydides Translated into English, With Introduction, Marginal Analysis, Notes, and Indices.* Oxford at the Clarendon Press. 1881.

PERICLES

ON THE ATHENIAN NATIONAL SPIRIT
(430 B.C.)

In the second year of the war, Pericles rallied a disheartened Athens: "Know that our city has the greatest name in all the world because she has never yielded to misfortunes, but has sacrificed more lives and endured severer hardships in war than any other; wherefore also she has the greatest power of any state up to this day; and the memory of her glory will always survive. Even if we should be compelled at last to abate somewhat of our greatness (for all things have their times of growth and decay), yet will the recollection live, that, of all Hellenes, we ruled over the greatest number of Hellenic subjects; that we withstood our enemies, whether single or united, in the most terrible wars, and that we were the inhabitants of a city endowed with every sort of wealth and greatness."

———————

[Thucydides' narrative:] *After the second Peloponnesian invasion, now that Attica had been once more ravaged, and the war and the plague together lay heavy upon the Athenians, a change came over their spirit. They blamed Pericles because he had persuaded them to go to war, declaring that he was the author of their troubles; and they were anxious to come to terms with the Lacedaemonians. Accordingly envoys were despatched to Sparta, but they met with no success. And now, being completely at their wits' end, they turned upon Pericles. He saw that they were exasperated by their misery and were behaving just as he had always anticipated that they would. And so, being still general, he called an assembly, wanting to encourage them and to convert their angry feelings into a gentler and more hopeful mood. At this assembly he came forward and spoke as follows:*

I was expecting this outburst of indignation; the causes of it are not unknown to me. And I have summoned an assembly that I may remind you of your resolutions and reprove you for your inconsiderate anger against me, and want of fortitude in misfortune. In my judgment it would be better for individuals themselves that the citizens should suffer and the state flourish than that the citizens should flourish and the state suffer. A private man, however successful in his own dealings, if his country perish is involved in her destruction; but if he be an unprosperous citizen of a prosperous city he is much more likely to recover. Seeing then that states can bear the misfortune of individuals, but individuals cannot bear the misfortunes of the state, let us all stand by our country and not do what you are doing now, who because you are stunned by your private calamities are letting go the hope of saving the state, and condemning not only me who advised, but yourselves who consented to, the war. Yet I with whom you are so angry venture to say of myself, that I am as capable as anyone of devising and explaining a sound policy; and that I am a lover of my country, and incorruptible.

Now a man may have a policy which he cannot clearly expound, and then he might as well have none at all; or he may possess both ability and eloquence, but if he is disloyal to his country he cannot, like a true man, speak in her interest; or again he may be unable to resist a bribe, and then all his other good qualities will be sold for money. If, when you determined to go to war, you believed me to have somewhat more of the statesman in me than others, it is not fair that I should now be charged with anything like crime.

I allow that for men who are in prosperity and free to choose it is great folly to make war. But when they must either submit and at once surrender independence, or strike and be free, then he who shuns and not he who meets the danger is deserving of blame. For my own part, I am the same man and stand where I did. But you are changed; for you have been driven by misfortune to recall the consent which you gave when you were yet unhurt, and to think that my advice was wrong because your own characters are weak. The pain is present and comes home to each of you, but the good is as yet unrealized by anyone; and your minds have not the strength to persevere in your resolution, now that a great reverse has overtaken you unawares. Anything which is sudden and unexpected and utterly beyond calculation, such a disaster for instance as this plague coming upon other misfortunes, enthralls the spirit of a man. Nevertheless, being the citizens of a great city and educated in a temper of greatness, you should not succumb to calamities however overwhelming, or darken the luster of your fame. For if men hate the presumption of those who claim a reputation to which they have no right, they equally condemn the faintheartedness of those who fall below the glory which is their own. You should lose the sense of your private sorrows and cling to the deliverance of the state.

As to your sufferings in the war, if you fear that they may be very great and after all fruitless, I have shown you already over and over again that such a fear is groundless. If you are still unsatisfied I will indicate one element of your superiority which appears to have escaped you, although it nearly touches your imperial greatness. I too have never mentioned it before, nor would I now, because the claim may seem too arrogant, if I did not see that you are unreasonably depressed. You think that your empire is confined to your allies, but I say that of the two divisions of the world accessible to man, the land and the sea, there is one of which you are absolute masters, and have, or may have, the dominion to any extent which you please. Neither the great king nor any nation on earth can hinder a navy like yours from penetrating whithersoever you choose to sail. When we reflect on this great power, houses and lands, of which the loss seems so dreadful to you, are as nothing. We ought not to be troubled about them, or to think much of them in comparison; they are only the garden of the house, the superfluous ornament of wealth; and you may be sure that if we cling to our freedom and preserve that, we shall soon enough recover all the rest. But, if we are the servants of others, we shall be sure to lose not only freedom, but all that freedom gives. And where your ancestors doubly succeeded, you will doubly fail. For their empire was not inherited by them from others but won by the labor of their hands, and by them preserved and bequeathed to us. And to be robbed of what you have is a greater disgrace than to attempt a conquest and fail.

Meet your enemies, therefore, not only with spirit, but with disdain. A coward or a fortunate fool may brag and vaunt, but he only is capable of disdain whose conviction that he is stronger than his enemy rests, like our own, on grounds of reason. Fighting in a fair field, courage is fortified by the intelligence which looks down upon an enemy; an intelligence relying, not on hope, which is the strength of helplessness, but on that surer foresight which is given by reason and observation of facts.

Once more, you are bound to maintain the imperial dignity of your city in which you all take pride; for you should not covet the glory unless you will endure the toil. And do not imagine that you are fighting about a simple issue, freedom or slavery; you have an empire to lose, and there is the danger to which the hatred of your imperial rule has exposed you. Neither can you resign your power, if, at this crisis, any timorous or inactive spirit is for thus playing the honest man. For by this time your empire has become a tyranny which in the opinion of mankind may have been unjustly gained, but which cannot be safely surrendered. The men of whom I was speaking, if they could find followers, would soon ruin a city, and if they were to go and found a state of their own, would equally ruin that. For inaction is secure only when arrayed by the side of activity; nor is it expedient or safe for a sovereign, but only for a subject state, to be a servant.

You must not be led away by the advice of such citizens as these, nor be angry with me; for the resolution in favor of war was your own as much as mine. What if the enemy has come and done what he was certain to do when you refused to yield? What too if the plague followed? That was an unexpected blow, but we might have foreseen all the rest. I am well aware that your hatred of me is aggravated by it. But how unjustly, unless to me you also ascribe the credit of any extraordinary success which may befall you! The visitations of heaven should be borne with resignation, the sufferings inflicted by an enemy with manliness. This has always been the spirit of Athens, and should not die out in you. Know that our city has the greatest name in all the world because she has never yielded to misfortunes, but has sacrificed more lives and endured severer hardships in war than any other; wherefore also she has the greatest power of any state up to this day; and the memory of her glory will always survive. Even if we should be compelled at last to abate somewhat of our greatness (for all things have their times of growth and decay), yet will the recollection live, that, of all Hellenes, we ruled over the greatest number of Hellenic subjects; that we withstood our enemies, whether single or united, in the most terrible wars, and that we were the inhabitants of a city endowed with every sort of wealth and greatness.

The indolent may indeed find fault, but the man of action will seek to rival us, and he who is less fortunate will envy us. To be hateful and offensive has ever been at the time the fate of those who have aspired to empire. But he judges well who accepts unpopularity in a great cause. Hatred does not last long, and, besides the immediate splendor of great actions, the renown of them endures forever in men's memories. Looking forward to such future glory and present avoidance of dishonor, make an effort now and secure both. Let no herald be sent to the Lacedaemonians, and do not let them know that you are made low by your sufferings. For those are the greatest states and the greatest men, who, when misfortunes come, are the least lowered in spirit and the most resolute in action.

[Thucydides' narrative:] *By these and similar words Pericles endeavored to appease the anger of the Athenians against himself, and to divert their minds from their terrible situation. In the conduct of public affairs they took his advice, and sent no more embassies to Sparta; they were again eager to prosecute the war. Yet in private they felt their sufferings keenly; the common people had been deprived even of the little which they possessed, while the upper class had lost fair estates in the country with all their houses and rich furniture. Worst of all, instead of enjoying peace, they were now at war. The popular indignation was not pacified until they had fined Pericles; but, soon afterwards, with the usual fickleness of a multitude, they elected him general and committed all their affairs to his charge. Their private sorrows were beginning to be less acutely felt, and for a time of public need they thought that there was no man like him. During the peace while he was at the head of affairs he ruled with prudence; under his guidance Athens was safe, and reached the height of her greatness in his time.*

When the war began he showed that here too he had formed a true estimate of the Athenian power. He survived the commencement of hostilities two years and six months; and, after his death, his foresight was even better appreciated than during his life. For he had told the Athenians that if they would be patient and would attend to their navy, and not seek to enlarge their dominion while the war was going on, nor imperil the existence of the city, they would be victorious; but they did all that he told them not to do, and in matters which seemingly had nothing to do with the war, from motives of private ambition and private interest they adopted a policy which had disastrous effects in respect both of themselves and of their allies; their measures, had they been successful, would only have brought honor and profit to individuals, and, when unsuccessful, crippled the city in the conduct of the war. The reason of the difference was that he, deriving authority from his capacity and acknowledged worth, being also a man of transparent integrity, was able to control the multitude in a free spirit; he led them rather than was led by them; for, not seeking power by dishonest arts, he had no need to say pleasant things, but, on the strength of his own high character, could venture to oppose and even to anger them.

When he saw them unseasonably elated and arrogant, his words humbled and awed them; and, when they were depressed by groundless fears, he sought to reanimate their confidence. Thus Athens, though still in name a democracy, was in fact ruled by her greatest citizen. But his successors were more on an equality with one another, and, each one struggling to be first himself, they were ready to sacrifice the whole conduct of affairs to the whims of the people. Such weakness in a great and imperial city led to many errors, of which the greatest was the Sicilian expedition; not that the Athenians miscalculated their enemy's power, but they themselves, instead of consulting for the interests of the expedition which they had sent out, were occupied in intriguing against one another for the leadership of the democracy, and not only hampered the operations of the army, but became embroiled, for the first time, at home. And yet after they had lost in the Sicilian expedition the greater part of their fleet and army, and were now distracted by revolution, still they held out three years, not only against their former enemies, but against the Sicilians who had combined with them, and against most of their own allies who had risen in revolt.

Even when Cyrus the son of the King joined in the war and supplied the Peloponnesian fleet with money, they continued to resist, and were at last overthrown, not by their enemies, but by themselves and their own internal dissensions. So that at the time Pericles was more than justified in the conviction at which his foresight had arrived, that the Athenians would win an easy victory over the unaided forces of the Peloponnesians.

SOURCE: Benjamin Jowett. *Thucydides Translated into English, With Introduction, Marginal Analysis, Notes, and Indices.* Oxford at the Clarendon Press. 1881.

CLEON Versus DIODOTUS

ON SENTENCING THE
MYTILENAEANS TO DEATH (427 B.C.)

In Athens, the war provoked a revenge-mission on the people of a former ally. When the Athenian assembly repented, a debate broke out between the wrathful Cleon (d. 422 B.C.) and the practical statesman Diodotus. H. D. F. Kitto describes Cleon's words as "A clever speech, with just enough truth in it to conceal, partially, its flattery of the vulgar and its encouragement of the violent—but one wonders if Cleon would have dared to speak like this in the presence of Pericles." (Pericles had died in 429 B.C.) Of Diodotus's more effective speech, Kitto adds: "We have no right to assume that Diodotus felt no emotion. The occasion, in his view, called for reason, not for emotion; he will meet Cleon not by displaying finer feelings but by using finer arguments. In this respect he is like Greek poetry and Greek art: the intellectual control of feeling increases the total effect."[1] Nothing is known of the admirable Diodotus outside of this episode in Thucydides.

[Thucydides' narrative:] *When the captives arrived at Athens the Athenians instantly put Salaethus to death, although he made various offers, and among other things promised to procure the withdrawal of the Peloponnesians from Plataea, which was still blockaded. Concerning the other captives a discussion was held, and in their indignation the Athenians*

---

[1] H. D. F. Kitto. *The Greeks*. Harmondsworth, England: Penguin. 1973. 145, 147.

determined to put to death not only the men then at Athens, but all the grown-up citizens of Mytilene, and to enslave the women and children; the act of the Mytilenaeans appeared inexcusable, because they were not subjects like the other states which had revolted, but free. That Peloponnesian ships should have had the audacity to find their way to Ionia and assist the rebels contributed to increase their fury; and the action showed that the revolt was a long premeditated affair. So they sent a trireme to Paches announcing their determination, and bidding him put the Mytilenaeans to death at once. But on the following day a kind of remorse seized them; they began to reflect that a decree which doomed to destruction not only the guilty, but a whole city, was cruel and monstrous. The Mytilenaean envoys who were at Athens perceived the change of feeling, and they and the Athenians who were in their interest prevailed on the magistrates to bring the question again before the people; this they were the more willing to do, because they saw themselves that the majority of the citizens were anxious to have an opportunity given them of reconsidering their decision. An assembly was again summoned, and different opinions were expressed by different speakers. In the former assembly, Cleon the son of Cleaenetus had carried the decree condemning the Mytilenaeans to death. He was the most violent of the citizens, and at that time exercised by far the greatest influence over the people. And now he came forward a second time and spoke as follows:

[Cleon]

I have remarked again and again that a democracy cannot manage an empire, but never more than now, when I see you regretting your condemnation of the Mytilenaeans. Having no fear or suspicion of one another in daily life, you deal with your allies upon the same principle, and you do not consider that whenever you yield to them out of pity or are misled by their specious tales, you are guilty of a weakness dangerous to yourselves, and receive no thanks from them. You should remember that your empire is a despotism exercised over unwilling subjects, who are always conspiring against you; they do not obey in return for any kindness which you do them to your own injury, but in so far as you are their masters; they have no love of you, but they are held down by force. Besides, what can be more detestable than to be perpetually changing our minds? We forget that a state in which the laws, though imperfect, are inviolable, is better off than one in which the laws are good but ineffective. Dullness and modesty are a more useful combination than cleverness and license; and the more simple sort generally make better citizens than the more astute. For the latter desire to be thought wiser than the laws; they want to be always getting their own way in public discussions; they think that they can nowhere have a finer opportunity of displaying their intelligence, and their folly generally ends in the ruin of their country; whereas the others, mistrusting their own capacity, admit that the laws are wiser than themselves: they do not pretend to criticize the arguments of a great speaker; and being impartial judges, not ambitious rivals, they hit the mark. That is the spirit in which we should act; not suffering ourselves to be so excited by our own cleverness in a war of wits as to advise the Athenian people contrary to our own better judgment.

I myself think as I did before, and I wonder at those who have brought forward the case of the Mytilenaeans again, thus interposing a delay which is in the interest of the evil-doer. For after a time the anger of the sufferer waxes dull, and he pursues the offender with less keenness; but the vengeance which follows closest upon the wrong is most adequate to it and exacts the fullest retribution. And again I wonder who will answer me, and whether he will attempt to show that the crimes of the Mytilenaeans are a benefit to us, or that when we suffer, our allies suffer with us. Clearly he must be someone who has such confidence in his powers of speech as to contend that you never adopted what was most certainly your resolution; or else he must be someone who, under the inspiration of a bribe, elaborates a sophistical speech in the hope of diverting you from the point. In such rhetorical contests the city gives away the prizes to others, while she takes the risk upon herself. And you are to blame, for you order these contests amiss. When speeches are to be heard, you are too fond of using your eyes, but, where actions are concerned, you trust your ears; you estimate the possibility of future enterprises from the eloquence of an orator, but as to accomplished facts, instead of accepting ocular demonstration, you believe only what ingenious critics tell you. No men are better dupes, sooner deceived by novel notions, or slower to follow approved advice. You despise what is familiar, while you are worshippers of every new extravagance. Not a man of you but would be an orator if he could; when he cannot, he will not yield the palm to a more successful rival: he would fain show that he does not let his wits come limping after, but that he can praise a sharp remark before it is well out of another's mouth; he would like to be as quick in anticipating what is said, as he is slow in foreseeing its consequences. You are always hankering after an ideal state, but you do not give your minds even to what is straight before you. In a word, you are at the mercy of your own ears, and sit like spectators attending a performance of sophists, but very unlike counselors of a state.

I want you to put aside this trifling, and therefore I say to you that no single city has ever injured us so deeply as Mytilene. I can excuse those who find our rule too heavy to bear, or who have revolted because the enemy has compelled them. But islanders who had walls, and were unassailable by our enemies, except at sea, and on that element were sufficiently protected by a fleet of their own, who were independent and treated by us with the highest regard, when they act thus, they have not revolted (that word would imply that they were oppressed), but they have rebelled, and entering the ranks of our bitterest enemies have conspired with them to seek our ruin. And surely this is far more atrocious than if they had been led by motives of ambition to take up arms against us on their own account. They learned nothing from the misfortunes of their neighbors who had already revolted and been subdued by us, nor did the happiness of which they were in the enjoyment make them hesitate to court destruction. They trusted recklessly to the future, and cherishing hopes which, if less than their wishes, were greater than their powers, they went to war, preferring might to right. No sooner did they seem likely to win than they set upon us, although we were doing them no wrong. Too swift and sudden a rise is apt to make cities insolent and, in general, ordinary good-fortune is safer than extraordinary. Mankind apparently find it easier to drive away adversity than to retain prosperity.

We should from the first have made no difference between the Mytilenaeans and the rest of our allies, and then their insolence would never have risen to such a height; for men naturally despise those who court them, but respect those who do not give way to them. Yet it is not too late to punish them as their crimes deserve. And do not absolve the people while you throw the blame upon the nobles. For they were all of one mind when we were to be attacked. Had the people deserted the nobles and come over to us, they might at this moment have been reinstated in their city; but they considered that their safety lay in sharing the dangers of the oligarchy, and therefore they joined in the revolt. Reflect: if you impose the same penalty upon those of your allies who willfully rebel and upon those who are constrained by the enemy, which of them will not revolt upon any pretext however trivial, seeing that, if he succeed, he will be free, and, if he fail, no irreparable evil will follow? We in the meantime shall have to risk our lives and our fortunes against everyone in turn. When conquerors we shall recover only a ruined city, and, for the future, the revenues which are our strength will be lost to us. But if we fail, the number of our adversaries will be increased. And when we ought to be employed in repelling the enemies with whom we have to do, we shall be wasting time in fighting against our own allies.

Do not then hold out a hope, which eloquence can secure or money buy, that they are to be excused and that their error is to be deemed human and venial. Their attack was not unpremeditated; that might have been an excuse for them; but they knew what they were doing. This was my original contention, and I still maintain that you should abide by your former decision, and not be misled either by pity, or by the charm of words, or by a too forgiving temper. There are no three things more prejudicial to your power. Mercy should be reserved for the merciful, and not thrown away upon those who will have no compassion on us, and who must by the force of circumstances always be our enemies. And our charming orators will still have an arena, but one in which the questions at stake will not be so grave, and the city will not pay so dearly for her brief pleasure in listening to them, while they for a good speech get a good fee.

Lastly, forgiveness is naturally shown to those who, being reconciled, will continue friends, and not to those who will always remain what they were, and will abate nothing of their enmity. In one word, if you do as I say, you will do what is just to the Mytilenaeans, and also what is expedient for yourselves; but, if you take the opposite course, they will not be grateful to you, and you will be self-condemned. For, if they were right in revolting, you must be wrong in maintaining your empire. But if, right or wrong, you are resolved to rule, then rightly or wrongly they must be chastised for your good. Otherwise you must give up your empire, and, when virtue is no longer dangerous, you may be as virtuous as you please.

Punish them as they would have punished you; let not those who have escaped appear to have less feeling than those who conspired against them. Consider: what might not they have been expected to do if they had conquered?—especially since they were the aggressors. For those who wantonly attack others always rush into extremes, and sometimes, like these Mytilenaeans, to their own destruction. They know the fate which is reserved for them by an enemy who is spared: when a man is injured wantonly he is more dangerous if he escape than the enemy who has only suffered what he has inflicted. Be true then to yourselves, and recall as vividly as you can what you felt at the time; think how you would have given the world to crush your enemies, and now take your revenge. Do not be soft-hearted at the sight of their distress, but remember the danger which was once hanging over your heads. Chastise them as they deserve, and prove by an example to your other allies that rebellion will be punished with death. If this is made quite clear to them, your attention will no longer be diverted from your enemies by wars against your own allies.

[Thucydides' narrative:] *Such were the words of Cleon; and after him Diodotus the son of Eucrates, who in the previous assembly had been the chief opponent of the decree which condemned the Mytilenaeans, came forward again and spoke as follows:*

[Diodotus]

I am far from blaming those who invite us to reconsider our sentence upon the Mytilenaeans, nor do I approve of the censure which has been cast on the practice of deliberating more than once about matters so critical. In my opinion the two things most adverse to good counsel are haste and passion; the former is generally a mark of folly, the latter of vulgarity and narrowness of mind. When a man insists that words ought not to be our guides in action, he is either wanting in sense or wanting in honesty: he is wanting in sense if he does not see that there is no other way in which we can throw light on the unknown future; and he is not honest if, seeking to carry a discreditable measure, and knowing that he cannot speak well in a bad cause, he reflects that he can slander well and terrify his opponents and his audience by the audacity of his calumnies. Worst of all are those who, besides other topics of abuse, declare that their opponent is hired to make an eloquent speech. If they accused him of stupidity only, when he failed in producing an impression, he might go his way having lost his reputation for sense but not for honesty; whereas he who is accused of dishonesty, even if he succeed, is viewed with suspicion, and, if he fail, is thought to be both fool and rogue. And so the city suffers; for she is robbed of her counselors by fear. Happy would she be if such citizens could not speak at all, for then the people would not be misled.

The good citizen should prove his superiority as a speaker, not by trying to intimidate those who are to follow him in debate, but by fair argument; and the wise city ought not to give increased honor to her best counselor, any more than she will deprive him of that which he has; while he whose proposal is rejected not only ought to receive no punishment, but should be free from all reproach. Then he who succeeds will not say pleasant things contrary to his better judgment in order to gain a still higher place in popular favor, and he who fails will not be striving to attract the multitude to himself by like compliances.

But we take an opposite course; and still worse. Even when we know a man to be giving the wisest counsel, a suspicion of corruption is set on foot; and from a jealousy which is perhaps groundless we allow the state to lose an undeniable advantage. It has come to this, that the best advice when offered in plain terms is as much distrusted as the worst; and not only he who wishes to lead the multitude into the most dangerous courses must deceive them, but he who speaks in the cause of right must make himself believed by lying. In this city, and in this city only, to do good openly and without deception is impossible, because you are too clever; and, when a man confers an unmistakable benefit on you, he is rewarded by a suspicion that, in some underhand manner, he gets more than he gives. But, whatever you may suspect, when great interests are at stake, we who advise ought to look further and weigh our words more carefully than you whose vision is limited. And you should remember that we are accountable for our advice to you, but you who listen are accountable to nobody. If he who gave and he who followed evil counsel suffered equally, you would be more reasonable in your ideas; but now, whenever you meet with a reverse, led away by the passion of the moment you punish the individual who is your adviser for his error of judgment, and your own error you condone, if the judgments of many concurred in it.

I do not come forward either as an advocate of the Mytilenaeans or as their accuser; the question for us rightly considered is not, what are their crimes? but, what is for our interest? If I prove them ever so guilty, I will not on that account bid you put them to death, unless it is expedient. Neither, if perchance there be some degree of excuse for them, would I have you spare them, unless it be clearly for the good of the state. For I conceive that we are now concerned, not with the present, but with the future. When Cleon insists that the infliction of death will be expedient and will secure you against revolt in time to come, I, like him taking the ground of future expediency, stoutly maintain the contrary position; and I would not have you be misled by the apparent fairness of his proposal, and reject the solid advantages of mine. You are angry with the Mytilenaeans, and the superior justice of his argument may for the moment attract you; but we are not at law with them, and do not want to be told what is just; we are considering a question of policy, and desire to know how we can turn them to account.

To many offences less than theirs states have affixed the punishment of death; nevertheless, excited by hope, men still risk their lives. No one when venturing on a perilous enterprise ever yet passed a sentence of failure on himself. And what city when entering on a revolt ever imagined that the power which she had, whether her own or obtained from her allies, did not justify the attempt? All are by nature prone to err both in public and in private life, and no law will prevent them.

Men have gone through the whole catalogue of penalties in the hope that, by increasing their severity, they may suffer less at the hands of evil-doers. In early ages the punishments, even of the worst offences, would naturally be milder; but as time went on and mankind continued to transgress, they seldom stopped short of death. And still there are transgressors. Some greater terror then has yet to be discovered; certainly death is no deterrent. For poverty inspires necessity with daring; and wealth engenders avarice in pride and insolence; and the various conditions of human life, as they severally fall under the sway of some mighty and fatal power, lure men through their passions to destruction. Desire and hope are never wanting, the one leading, the other following, the one devising the enterprise, the other suggesting that fortune will be kind; and they are the most ruinous, for, being unseen, they far outweigh the dangers which are seen. Fortune too assists the illusion, for she often presents herself unexpectedly, and induces states as well as individuals to run into peril, however inadequate their means; and states even more than individuals, because they are throwing for a higher stake, freedom and empire, and because when a man has a whole people acting with him, he magnifies himself out of all reason. In a word then, it is impossible and simply absurd to suppose that human nature when bent upon some favorite project can be restrained either by the strength of law or by any other terror.

We ought not therefore to act hastily out of a mistaken reliance on the security which the penalty of death affords. Nor should we drive our rebellious subjects to despair; they must not think that there is no place for repentance, or that they may not at any moment give up their mistaken policy. Consider: at present, although a city may actually have revolted, when she becomes conscious of her weakness she will capitulate while still able to defray the cost of the war and to pay tribute for the future; but if we are too severe, will not the citizens make better preparations, and, when besieged, resist to the last, knowing that it is all the same whether they come to terms early or late? Shall not we ourselves suffer? For we shall waste our money by sitting down before a city which refuses to surrender; when the place is taken it will be a mere wreck, and we shall in future lose the revenues derived from it; and in these revenues lies our military strength.

Do not then weigh offences with the severity of a judge, when you will only be injuring yourselves, but have an eye to the future; let the penalties which you impose on rebellious cities be moderate, and then their wealth will be undiminished and at your service. Do not hope to find a safeguard in the severity of your laws, but only in the vigilance of your administration. At present we do just the opposite; a free people under a strong government will always revolt in the hope of independence; and when we have put them down we think that they cannot be punished too severely. But instead of inflicting extreme penalties on free men who revolt, we should practice extreme vigilance before they revolt, and never allow such a thought to enter their minds. When however they have been once put down we ought to extenuate their crimes as much as possible.

Think of another great error into which you would fall if you listened to Cleon. At present the popular party are everywhere our friends; either they do not join with the oligarchs, or, if compelled to do so, they are always ready to turn against the authors of the revolt; and so in going to war with a rebellious state you have the multitude on your side. But, if you destroy the people of Mytilene who took no part in the revolt, and who voluntarily surrendered the city as soon as they got arms into their hands; in the first place they were your benefactors, and to slay them would be a crime; in the second place you will play into the hands of the oligarchic parties, who henceforward, in fomenting a revolt, will at once have the people on their side; for you will have proclaimed to all that the innocent and the guilty will share the same fate. Even if they were guilty you should wink at their conduct, and not allow the only friends whom you have left to be converted into enemies.

Far more conducive to the maintenance of our empire would it be to suffer wrong willingly, than for the sake of justice to put to death those whom we had better spare. Cleon may speak of a punishment which is just and also expedient, but you will find that, in any proposal like his, the two cannot be combined.

Assured then that what I advise is for the best, and yielding neither to pity nor to lenity, for I am as unwilling as Cleon can be that you should be influenced by any such motives, but simply weighing the arguments which I have urged, accede to my proposal: Pass sentence at your leisure on the Mytilenaeans whom Paches, deeming them guilty, has sent hither; but leave the rest of the inhabitants where they are. This will be good policy for the future, and will strike present terror into your enemies. For wise counsel is really more formidable to an enemy than the severity of unreasoning violence.

[Thucydides' narrative:] *Thus spoke Diodotus, and such were the proposals on either side which most nearly represented the opposing parties. In spite of the reaction, there was a struggle between the two opinions; the show of hands was very near, but the motion of Diodotus prevailed. The Athenians instantly despatched another trireme, hoping that, if the second could overtake the first, which had a start of about twenty-four hours, it might be in time to save the city. The Mytilenaean envoys provided wine and barley for the crew, and promised them great rewards if they arrived first. And such was their energy that they continued rowing whilst they ate their barley, kneaded with wine and oil, and slept and rowed by turns. Fortunately no adverse wind sprang up, and, the first of the two ships sailing in no great hurry on her untoward errand, and the second hastening as I have described, the one did indeed arrive sooner than the other, but not much sooner. Paches had read the decree and was about to put it into execution, when the second appeared and arrested the fate of the city.*

So near was Mytilene to destruction.

SOURCE: Benjamin Jowett. *Thucydides Translated into English, With Introduction, Marginal Analysis, Notes, and Indices.* Oxford at the Clarendon Press. 1881.

ALCIBIADES Versus NICIAS

ON THE ATHENIAN EXPEDITION
TO SICILY (414 B.C.)

Alcibiades (c. 450–404 B.C.) was the dynamic, brilliant wonder of
Athens, who, as a cocky youth, only allowed himself to be
restrained by the great philosopher and teacher Socrates. He thrived
and delighted in activity and competition. Plutarch observes:"He
had great advantages for entering public life; his noble birth, his
riches, the personal courage he had shown in divers battles, and the
multitude of his friends and dependents, threw open, so to say,
folding-doors for his admittance. But he did not consent to let his
power with the people rest on anything rather than his own gift of
eloquence."[1] In the midst of the Peloponnesian War, jealous of the
influence of the great general Nicias (d. 413 B.C.), who was more
reasonably cautious, Alcibiades advocated an attack on the distant
island of Sicily. "Dazzled by the charm and brilliance of Alcibiades,
the darling and evil genius of the democracy, the Athenians, despite
of the treaty, engaged in hostilities against Sparta and her allies,"
writes Bernard Knox; "worse still, in 415, they sent a powerful
expedition—'No armament so magnificent or costly had ever been
sent out by any single Greek power,' says Thucydides—against the
rich Sicilian city of Syracuse. 'By adding Sicily to our empire,'
Alcibiades told them, 'we shall probably become masters of all
Greece.' The campaign was a disaster . . . Sparta and her allies now

---

[1] *The Lives of the Nobel Grecians and Romans*. Translated by John Dryden. Revised by
Arthur Hugh Clough. New York: Modern Library (Random House). 1932. 239.

took the offensive, and though it took them another seven years, they forced Athens to surrender in 404."[2]

———⚬———

[Thucydides' narrative:] *Most of the Athenians who came forward to speak were in favor of war, and reluctant to rescind the vote which had been already passed, although a few took the other side. The most enthusiastic supporter of the expedition was Alcibiades the son of Cleinias; he was determined to oppose Nicias, who was always his political enemy and had just now spoken of him in disparaging terms; but the desire to command was even a stronger motive with him. He was hoping that he might be the conqueror of Sicily and Carthage; and that success would repair his private fortunes, and gain him money as well as glory. He had a great position among the citizens and was devoted to horseracing and other pleasures which outran his means. And in the end his wild courses went far to ruin the Athenian state. For the people feared the extremes to which he carried the lawlessness of his personal habits, and the far-reaching purposes which invariably animated him in all his actions. They thought that he was aiming at a tyranny and set themselves against him. And therefore, although his talents as a military commander were unrivalled, they entrusted the administration of the war to others, because they personally objected to his private habits; and so they speedily shipwrecked the state. He now came forward and spoke as follows:*

[Alcibiades]

I have a better right to command, men of Athens, than another; for as Nicias has attacked me, I must begin by praising myself; and I consider that I am worthy. Those doings of mine for which I am so much cried out against are an honor to myself and to my ancestors, and a solid advantage to my country. In consequence of the distinguished manner in which I represented the state at Olympia, the other Hellenes formed an idea of our power which even exceeded the reality, although they had previously imagined that we were exhausted by war. I sent into the lists seven chariots,—no other private man ever did the like; I was victor, and also won the

---

[2]Bernard Knox. *Backing into the Future: The Classical Tradition and Its Renewal.* New York: W. W. Norton and Company. 1994. 151.

second and fourth prize; and I ordered everything in a style worthy of my victory. Apart from the conventional honor paid to such successes, the energy which is shown by them creates an impression of power. At home, again, whenever I gain distinction by providing choruses or by the performance of some other public duty, although the citizens are naturally jealous of me, to strangers these acts of munificence are a new argument of our strength.

There is some use in the folly of a man who at his own cost benefits not only himself, but the state. And where is the injustice, if I or anyone who feels his own superiority to another refuses to be on a level with him? The unfortunate keep their misfortunes to themselves. We do not expect to be recognized by our acquaintance when we are down in the world; and on the same principle why should anyone complain when treated with disdain by the more fortunate? He who would have proper respect shown to him should himself show it towards others. I know that men of this lofty spirit, and all who have been in any way illustrious, are hated while they are alive, by their equals especially, and in a lesser degree by others who have to do with them; but that they leave behind them to after-ages a reputation which leads even those who are not of their family to claim kindred with them, and that they are the glory of their country, which regards them, not as aliens or as evil-doers, but as her own children, of whose character she is proud. These are my own aspirations, and this is the reason why my private life is assailed; but let me ask you, whether in the management of public affairs any man surpasses me. Did I not, without involving you in any great danger or expense, combine the most powerful states of Peloponnesus against the Lacedaemonians, whom I compelled to stake at Mantinea all that they had upon the fortune of one day? And even to this hour, although they were victorious in the battle, they have hardly recovered courage.

These were the achievements of my youth, and of what is supposed to be my monstrous folly; thus did I by winning words conciliate the Peloponnesian powers, and my heartiness made them believe in me and follow me. And now do not be afraid of me because I am young, but while I am in the flower of my days and Nicias enjoys the reputation of success, use the services of us both.

Having determined to sail, do not change your minds under the impression that Sicily is a great power. For although the Sicilian cities are populous, their inhabitants are a mixed multitude, and they readily give up old forms of government and receive new ones from without. No one really feels that he has a city of his own; and so the individual is ill provided with arms, and the country has no regular means of defense. A man looks only to what he can win from the common stock by arts of speech or by party violence; hoping, if he is overthrown, at any rate to carry off his prize and enjoy it elsewhere. They are a motley crew who are never of one mind in counsel and are incapable of any concert in action. Every man is for himself, and will readily come over to anyone who makes an attractive offer; the more readily if, as report says, they are in a state of internal discord. They boast of their hoplites, but, as has proved to be the case in all Hellenic states, the number of them is grossly exaggerated. Hellas has been singularly mistaken about her heavy infantry; and even in this war it was as much as she could do to collect enough of them.

The obstacles then which will meet us in Sicily, judging of them from the information which I have received, are not great; indeed, I have overrated them, for there will be many barbarians who, through fear of the Syracusans, will join us in attacking them. And at home there is nothing which, viewed rightly, need interfere with the expedition. Our forefathers had the same enemies whom we are now told that we are leaving behind us, and the Persian besides; but their strength lay in the greatness of their navy, and by that and that alone they gained their empire. Never were the Peloponnesians more hopeless of success than at the present moment; and let them be ever so confident, they will only invade us by land, which they can equally do whether we go to Sicily or not. But on the sea they cannot hurt us, for we shall leave behind us a navy equal to theirs.

What reason can we give to ourselves for hesitation? What excuse can we make to our allies for denying them aid? We have sworn to them, and have no right to argue that they never assisted us. In seeking their alliance we did not intend that they should come and help us here, but that they should harass our enemies in Sicily, and prevent them from coming hither. Like all other imperial powers, we have acquired our dominion by our readiness to assist anyone, whether Barbarian or Hellene, who may have invoked our aid. If we are all to sit and do nothing, or to draw distinctions of race when our help is requested, we shall add little to our empire, and run a great risk of losing it altogether. For

mankind do not await the attack of a superior power, they anticipate it. We cannot cut down an empire as we might a household;
but having once gained our present position, we must, while keeping a firm hold upon some, contrive occasion against others; for if
we are not rulers we shall be subjects.

You cannot afford to regard inaction in the same light as others
might, unless you impose a corresponding restriction on your practice. Convinced then that we shall be most likely to increase our
power here if we attack our enemies there, let us sail. We shall
humble the pride of the Peloponnesians when they see that, scorn-
ing the delights of repose, we have attacked Sicily. By the help of
our acquisitions there, we shall probably become masters of all
Hellas; at any rate we shall injure the Syracusans, and at the same
time benefit ourselves and our allies. Whether we succeed and
remain, or depart, in either case our navy will ensure our safety; for
at sea we shall be more than a match for all Sicily.

Nicias must not divert you from your purpose by preaching
indolence, and by trying to set the young against the old; rather
in your accustomed order, old and young taking counsel
together, after the manner of your fathers who raised Athens to
this height of greatness, strive to rise yet higher. Consider that
youth and age have no power unless united; but that the shal-
lower and the more exact and the middle sort of judgment, when
duly attempered, are likely to be most efficient. The state, if at
rest, like everything else will wear herself out by internal friction.
Every pursuit which requires skill will tend to decay, whereas by
conflict the city will always be gaining fresh experience and
learning to defend herself, not in theory, but in practice. My
opinion in short is, that a state used to activity will quickly be
ruined by the change to inaction; and that they of all men enjoy
the greatest security who are truest to themselves and their institutions even when they are not the best.

[Thucydides' narrative:] *Such were the words of Alcibiades. After hearing
him and the Egestaeans and certain Leontine exiles who came forward and
earnestly entreated assistance, reminding the Athenians of the oaths which
they had sworn, the people were more than ever resolved upon war. Nicias,
seeing that his old argument would no longer deter them, but that he might
possibly change their minds if he insisted on the magnitude of the force which
would be required, came forward again and spoke as follows:*

[Nicias]

Men of Athens, as I see that you are thoroughly determined to go to war, I accept the decision, and will advise you accordingly, trusting that the event will be such as we all wish. The cities which we are about to attack are, I am informed, powerful, and independent of one another; they are not inhabited by slaves, who would gladly pass out of a harder into an easier condition of life; and they are very unlikely to accept our rule in exchange for their present liberty. As regards numbers, although Sicily is but one island, it contains a great many Hellenic states. Not including Naxos and Catana (of which the inhabitants, as I hope, will be our allies because they are the kinsmen of the Leontines), there are seven other cities fully provided with means of warfare similar to our own, above all Selinus and Syracuse, the cities against which our expedition is particularly directed. For they have numerous hoplites, archers, and javelin-men, and they have many triremes which their large population will enable them to man; besides their private wealth, they have the treasures of the Selinuntian temples; and the Syracusans receive a tribute which has been paid them from time immemorial by certain barbarian tribes. Moreover, they have a numerous cavalry, and grow their own corn instead of importing it: in the two last respects they have a great advantage over us.

Against such a power more is needed than an insignificant force of marines; if we mean to do justice to our design, and not to be kept within our lines by the numbers of their cavalry, we must embark a multitude of infantry. For what if the Sicilians in terror combine against us, and we make no friends except the Egestaeans who can furnish us with horsemen capable of opposing theirs? To be driven from the island or to send for reinforcements, because we were wanting in forethought at first, would be disgraceful. We must take a powerful armament with us from home, in the full knowledge that we are going to a distant land, and that the expedition will be of a kind very different from any which you have hitherto made among your subjects against some enemy in this part of the world, yourselves the allies of others. Here a friendly country is always near, and you can easily obtain supplies. There you will be dependent on a country which is entirely strange to you, and whence during the four winter months hardly even a message can be sent hither.

I say, therefore, that we must take with us a large heavy-armed force both of Athenians and of allies, whether our own subjects or any Peloponnesians whom we can persuade or attract by pay to our service; also plenty of archers and javelin-men to act against the enemy's cavalry. Our naval superiority must be overwhelming, that we may not only be able to fight, but may have no difficulty in bringing in supplies. And there is the food carried from home, such as wheat and parched barley, which will have to be conveyed in merchant-vessels; we must also have bakers, drafted in a certain proportion from each mill, who will receive pay, but will be forced to serve, in order that, if we should be detained by a calm, the army may not want food; for it is not every city that will be able to receive so large a force as ours. We must make our preparations as complete as possible, and not be at the mercy of others; above all, we must take out with us as much money as we can; for as to the supplies of the Egestaeans which are said to be awaiting us, we had better assume that they are imaginary.

Even supposing we leave Athens with a force of our own, not merely equal to that of the enemy, but in every way superior, except indeed as regards the number of hoplites which they can put into the field, for in that respect equality is impossible, still it will be no easy task to conquer Sicily, or indeed to preserve ourselves. You ought to consider that we are like men going to found a city in a land of strangers and enemies, who on the very day of their disembarkation must have command of the country; for if they meet with a disaster they will have no friends. And this is what I fear. We shall have much need of prudence; still more of good fortune (and who can guarantee this to mortals?). Wherefore I would trust myself and the expedition, as little as possible to accident, and would not sail until I had taken such precautions as will be likely to ensure our safety. This I conceive to be the course which is the most prudent for the whole state, and, for us who are sent upon the expedition, a condition of safety. If anyone thinks otherwise, to him I resign the command.

[Thucydides' narrative:] *These were the words of Nicias. He meant either to deter the Athenians by bringing home to them the vastness of the undertaking, or to provide as far as he could for the security of the expedition if he were compelled to proceed. The result disappointed him. Far from losing their enthusiasm at the disagreeable prospect, they were more determined than ever; they approved of his advice, and were confident that every chance of danger was now removed. All alike were seized with a passionate desire to sail, the elder among them convinced that they would achieve the conquest of Sicily,—at any rate such an armament could suffer no disaster; the youth were longing to see with their own eyes the marvels of a distant land, and were confident of a safe return; the main body of the troops expected to receive present pay, and to conquer a country which would be an inexhaustible mine of pay for the future. The enthusiasm of the majority was so overwhelming that, although some disapproved, they were afraid of being thought unpatriotic if they voted on the other side, and therefore held their peace.*

SOURCE: Benjamin Jowett. *Thucydides Translated into English, With Introduction, Marginal Analysis, Notes, and Indices.* Oxford at the Clarendon Press. 1881.

XENOPHON

THE MARCH UP COUNTRY (401 B.C.)

Xenophon (c. 430–c. 354 B.C.) was born near Athens and was a student of Socrates. As a young man, shortly after the conclusion of the Peloponnesian War, he accompanied a friend who had been hired with ten thousand other Greek warriors by Cyrus, the brother of the King of Persia, Artaxerxes. Cyrus used the Greeks to attack his brother, and while the Greeks won the battle, Cyrus himself was killed. Soon after, the Greek generals of the mercenaries were tricked and put to death. The Persians expected the Greek soldiers to surrender, but instead, as we learn from Xenophon's remarkable story, *The Anabasis* (or "The March Up Country"), the Greeks, led now by Xenophon and four other elected generals, made their way out of Asia back home. The Roman orator Quintilian sings the praises of Xenophon's writing: "Why should I speak of the unaffected charm of Xenophon, so far beyond the power of affectation to attain? The Graces themselves seem to have molded his style, and we may with the utmost justice say of him, what the writer of the old comedy said of Pericles, that the goddess of persuasion sat enthroned upon his lips."[1] The following episode, describing Xenophon's first speech as a general, is from Book 3, Part 2.

---

[1] *The Works of Xenophon: Hellenica, Books I & II, and Anabasis*. Translated by H. G. Dakyns. London: Macmillan and Company. 1890.

[Xenophon's narrative:] *By the time the new generals had been chosen, the first faint glimmer of dawn had hardly commenced, as they met in the center of the camp, and resolved to post an advance guard and to call a general meeting of the soldiers. Now, when these had come together, Cheirisophus the Lacedaemonian first rose and spoke as follows: "Fellow-soldiers, the present posture of affairs is not pleasant, seeing that we are robbed of so many generals and captains and soldiers; and more than that, our former allies, Ariaeus and his men, have betrayed us; still, we must rise above our circumstances to prove ourselves brave men, and not give in, but try to save ourselves by glorious victory if we can; or, if not, at least to die gloriously, and never, while we have breath in our bodies, fall into the hands of our enemies. In which latter case, I fear, we shall suffer things, which I pray the gods may visit rather upon those we hate."*

At this point Cleanor the Ochomenian stood up and spoke as follows: "You see, men, the perjury and the impiety of the king. You see the faith-lessness of Tissaphernes, professing that he was next-door neighbor to Hellas, and would give a good deal to save us, in confirmation of which he took an oath to us himself, he gave us the pledge of his right hand, and then, with a lie upon his lips, this same man turned round and arrested our generals. He had no reverence even for Zeus, the god of strangers; but, after entertaining Clearchus at his own board as a friend, he used his hospitality to delude and decoy his victims. And Ariaeus, whom we offered to make king, with whom we exchanged pledges not to betray each other, even this man, without a particle of fear of the gods, or respect for Cyrus in his grave, though he was most honored by Cyrus in lifetime, even he has turned aside to the worst foes of Cyrus, and is doing his best to injure the dead man's friends. Them may the gods requite as they deserve! But we, with these things before our eyes, will not any more be cheated and cajoled by them; we will make the best fight we can, and having made it, whatever the gods think fit to send, we will accept."

After him Xenophon arose; he was arrayed for war in his bravest apparel: "For," said he to himself, "if the gods grant victory, the finest attire will match with victory best; or if I must needs die, then for one who has aspired to the noblest, it is well there should be some outward correspondence between his expectation and his end." He began his speech as follows:

Cleanor has spoken of the perjury and faithlessness of the barbarians, and you yourselves know them only too well, I fancy. If then we are minded to enter a second time into terms of friendship with them, with the experience of what our generals, who in all confidence entrusted themselves to their power, have suffered, reason would we should feel deep despondency. If, on the other hand, we purpose to take our good swords in our hands and to inflict punishment on them for what they have done, and from this time forward will be on terms of downright war with them, then, God helping, we have many a bright hope of safety.

[Xenophon's narrative:] *The words were scarcely spoken when someone sneezed,[2] and with one impulse the soldiers bowed in worship; and Xenophon proceeded:*

I propose, sirs, since, even as we spoke of safety, an omen from Zeus the Savior has appeared, we vow a vow to sacrifice to the Savior thank-offerings for safe deliverance, wheresoever first we reach a friendly country; and let us couple with that vow another of individual assent, that we will offer to the rest of the gods "according to our ability." Let all those who are in favor of this proposal hold up their hands.

[Xenophon's narrative:] *They all held up their hands, and there and then they vowed a vow and chanted the battle hymn. But as soon as these sacred matters were duly ended, he began once more thus:*

I was saying that many and bright are the hopes we have of safety. First of all, we it is who confirm and ratify the oaths we take by heaven, but our enemies have taken false oaths and broken the truce, contrary to their solemn word. This being so, it is but natural that the gods should be opposed to our enemies, but with ourselves allied; the gods, who are able to make the great ones quickly small, and out of sore perplexity can save the little ones with ease, what time it pleases them. In the next place, let me recall to your minds the dangers of our own forefathers, that you may see and know that bravery is your heirloom, and that by the aid of the gods brave men are rescued even out of the midst of sorest straits. So was it when the Persians came, and their attendant hosts, with a very great armament, to wipe out Athens from the face of the earth—the men of Athens had the heart to withstand them and conquered them. Then

---

[2]As in *The Odyssey*, the sneeze seemed to be a favorable sign from the gods.

they vowed to Artemis that for every man they slew of the enemy, they would sacrifice to the goddess goats so many; and when they could not find sufficient for the slain, they resolved to offer yearly five hundred; and to this day they perform that sacrifice. And at a somewhat later date, when Xerxes assembled his countless hosts and marched upon Hellas, then too our fathers conquered the forefathers of our foes by land and by sea.

And proofs of these things are yet to be seen in trophies; but the greatest witness of all is the freedom of our cities—the liberty of that land in which you were born and bred. For you call no man master or lord; you bow your heads to none save to the gods alone. Such were your forefathers, and you are their sons. Think not I am going to say that you put to shame in any way your ancestry—far from it. Not many days since, you too were drawn up in battle face to face with these true descendants of their ancestors, and by the help of heaven you conquered them, though they many times outnumbered you. At that time, it was to win a throne for Cyrus that you showed your bravery; today, when the struggle is for your own salvation, what is more natural than that you should show yourselves braver and more zealous still. Nay, it is very meet and right that you should be more undaunted still today to face the foe. The other day, though you had not tested them, and before your eyes lay their immeasurable host, you had the heart to go against them with the spirit of your fathers. Today you have made trial of them, and knowing that, however many times your number, they do not care to await your onset, what concern have you now to be afraid of them?

Nor let anyone suppose that herein is a point of weakness, in that Cyrus's troops, who before were drawn up by your side, have now deserted us, for they are even worse cowards still than those we worsted. At any rate they have deserted us, and sought refuge with them. Leaders of the forlorn hope of flight—far better is it to have them brigaded with the enemy than shoulder to shoulder in our ranks. But if any of you is out of heart to think that we have no cavalry, while the enemy have many squadrons to command, lay to heart this doctrine, that ten thousand horse only equal ten thousand men upon their backs, neither less nor more. Did anyone ever die in battle from the bite or kick of a horse? It is the men, the real swordsmen, who do whatever is done in battles. In fact we, on our stout shanks, are better mounted than those cavalry fellows; there they hang on to their horses' necks in mortal dread, not only of us, but of falling off; while we, well planted upon earth, can deal far heavier blows to our assailants, and aim more steadily at who we will. There is one point, I admit, in which their cavalry have the whiphand of us; it is safer for them than it is for us to run away.

Perhaps, however, you are in good heart about the fighting, but annoyed to think that Tissaphernes will not guide us any more, and that the king will not furnish us with a market any longer. Now, consider, is it better for us to have a guide like Tissaphernes, whom we know to be plotting against us, or to take our chance of the stray people whom we catch and compel to guide us, who will know that any mistake made in leading us will be a sad mistake for their own lives? Again, is it better to be buying provisions in a market of their providing, in scant measure and at high prices, without even the money to pay for them any longer; or, by right of conquest, to help ourselves, applying such measure as suits our fancy best?

Or again, perhaps you admit that our present position is not without its advantages, but you feel sure that the rivers are a difficulty, and think that you were never more taken in than when you crossed them; if so, consider whether, after all, this is not perhaps the most foolish thing which the barbarians have done. No river is impassable throughout; whatever difficulties it may present at some distance from its source, you need only make your way up to the springhead, and there you may cross it without wetting more than your ankles. But, granted that the rivers do bar our passage, and that guides are not forthcoming, what care we? We need feel no alarm for all that. We have heard of the Mysians, a people whom we certainly cannot admit to be better than ourselves; and yet they inhabit numbers of large and prosperous cities in the king's own country without asking leave. The Pisidians are an equally good instance, or the Lycaonians. We have seen with our own eyes how they fare: seizing fortresses down in the plains, and reaping the fruits of these men's territory. As to us, I go so far as to assert, we ought never to have let it be seen that we were bent on getting home: at any rate, not so soon; we should have begun stocking and furnishing ourselves, as if we fully meant to settle down for life somewhere or other hereabouts. I am sure that the king would be thrice glad to give the Mysians as many guides as they like, or as many hostages as they care to demand, in return for a safe conduct out of his country; he would make carriage roads for them, and if they preferred to take their departure in coaches and four, he would not say them nay. So too, I am sure, he would be only too glad to accommodate us in the same way, if he saw us preparing to settle down here. But, perhaps, it is just as well that we did not stop; for I fear, if once we learn to live in idleness and to batten in luxury and dalliance with these tall and handsome Median and Persian women and maidens, we shall be like the Lotus-eaters, and forget the road home altogether.

It seems to me that it is only right, in the first instance, to make an effort to return to Hellas and to revisit our hearths and homes, if only to prove to other Hellenes that it is their own faults if they are poor and needy, seeing it is in their power to give to those now living a pauper life at home a free passage hither, and convert them into well-to-do burghers at once. Now, sirs, is it not clear that all these good things belong to whoever has strength to hold them?

Let us look another matter in the face. How are we to march most safely? Or where blows are needed, how are we to fight to the best advantage? That is the question.

The first thing which I recommend is to burn the wagons we have got, so that we may be free to march wherever the army needs, and not, practically, make our baggage train our general. And, next, we should throw our tents into the bonfire also: for these again are only a trouble to carry, and do not contribute one grain of good either for fighting or getting provisions. Further, let us get rid of all superfluous baggage, save only what we require for the sake of war, or meat and drink, so that as many of us as possible may be under arms, and as few as possible doing porterage. I need not remind you that, in case of defeat, the owners' goods are not their own; but if we master our foes, we will make them our baggage bearers.

It only rests for me to name the one thing which I look upon as the greatest of all. You see, the enemy did not dare to bring war to bear upon us until they had first seized our generals; they felt that whilst our rulers were there, and we obeyed them, they were no match for us in war; but having got hold of them, they fully expected that the consequent confusion and anarchy would prove fatal to us. What follows? This: Officers and leaders ought to be more vigilant even than their predecessors; subordinates still more orderly and obedient to those in command now than even they were to those who are gone. And you should pass a resolution that, in case of insubordination, anyone who stands by is to aid the officer in chastising the offender. So the enemy will be mightily deceived; for on this day they will behold ten thousand Clearchuses instead of one, who will not suffer one man to play the coward. And now it is high time I brought my remarks to an end, for maybe the enemy will be here anon. Let those who are in favor of these proposals confirm them with all speed, that they may be realized in fact; or if any other course seem better, let not anyone, even though he be a private soldier, shrink from proposing it. Our common safety is our common need.

[Xenophon's narrative:] *After this Cheirisophus spoke. He said: "If there is anything else to be done, beyond what Xenophon has mentioned, we shall be able to carry it out presently; but with regard to what he has already proposed, it seems to me the best course to vote upon the matters at once. Those who are in favor of Xenophon's proposals, hold up their hands." They all held them up. Xenophon rose again and said:*

Listen, sirs, while I tell you what I think we have need of besides. It is clear that we must march where we can get provisions. Now, I am told there are some splendid villages not more than two miles and a half distant. I should not be surprised, then, if the enemy were to hang on our heels and dog us as we retire, like cowardly curs which rush out at the passer-by and bite him if they can, but when you turn upon them they run away. Such will be their tactics, I take it. It may be safer, then, to march in a hollow square, so as to place the baggage animals and our mob of sutlers in greater security. It will save time to make the appointments at once, and to settle who leads the square and directs the vanguard; who will take command of the two flanks, and who of the rearguard; so that, when the enemy appears, we shall not need to deliberate, but can at once set in motion the machinery in existence.

If anyone has any better plan, we need not adopt mine; but if not, suppose Cheirisophus takes the lead, as he is a Lacedaemonian, and the two eldest generals take in charge the two wings respectively, whilst Timasion and I, the two youngest, will for the present guard the rear. For the rest, we can but make experiment of this arrangement, and alter it with deliberation, as from time to time any improvement suggests itself. If anyone has a better plan to propose, let him do so.

[Xenophon's narrative:] *No dissentient voice was heard. Accordingly he said: "Those in favor of this resolution, hold up their hands." The resolution was carried.*

And now . . . it would be well to separate and carry out what we have decreed. If any of you has set his heart on seeing his friends again, let him remember to prove himself a man; there is no other way to achieve his heart's wish. Or is mere living an object with any of you, strive to conquer; if to slay is the privilege of victory, to die is the doom of the defeated. Or perhaps to gain money and wealth is your ambition, strive again for mastery; have not conquerors the double gain of keeping what is their own, whilst they seize the possessions of the vanquished?

SOURCE: *The Works of Xenophon: Hellenica, Books I & II, and Anabasis.* Translated by H. G. Dakyns. London: Macmillan and Company. 1890.

SOCRATES

THE APOLOGY (399 B.C.)

Socrates (469–399 B.C.) is the Athenian philosopher we know so well through the works of his pupil, the philosopher Plato (427–347 B.C.). Socrates' glorious, irrefutable, cleverly plain–spoken masterpiece was written up by Plato, who attended the trial. Socrates declares: ". . . from me you shall hear the whole truth: not, however, delivered after their manner in a set oration duly ornamented with words and phrases. No, by heaven! but I shall use the words and arguments which occur to me at the moment; for I am confident in the justice of my cause . . ." The speech's authenticity seems assured: "*[The] Apology* was written for an Athenian public that included many of the 501 jurors who had heard Socrates speak as well as many of the numerous spectators."[1] The prosecution charged Socrates with irreligion and corrupting the morals of young men through his teachings. Athens had lost the Peloponnesian war in 404 and among those considered blameworthy were Socrates' former students Alcibiades and Critias. In his defense, Socrates stated at the trial's conclusion that rather than accept exile, he chose execution, the fate argued for by the prosecution: "For the fear of death is indeed the pretence of wisdom, and not real wisdom, being a pretence of knowing the unknown; and no one knows whether death, which men in their fear apprehend to be the greatest evil, may not be the greatest good. Is not this ignorance of a disgraceful sort, the ignorance which is the conceit that a man

---

[1]Bernard Knox. *Backing into the Future: The Classical Tradition and Its Renewal.* New York: W. W. Norton and Company. 1994. 159.

60

knows what he does not know? And in this respect only I believe
myself to differ from men in general, and may perhaps claim to be
wiser than they are:—that whereas I know but little of the world
below, I do not suppose that I know . . ."

How you, O Athenians, have been affected by my accusers, I cannot tell; but I know that they almost made me forget who I was—
so persuasively did they speak; and yet they have hardly uttered a
word of truth. But of the many falsehoods told by them, there was
one which quite amazed me;—I mean when they said that you
should be upon your guard and not allow yourselves to be deceived
by the force of my eloquence. To say this, when they were certain
to be detected as soon as I opened my lips and proved myself to be
anything but a great speaker, did indeed appear to me most shameless—unless by the force of eloquence they mean the force of truth;
for if such is their meaning, I admit that I am eloquent. But in how
different a way from theirs!

Well, as I was saying, they have scarcely spoken the truth at all;
but from me you shall hear the whole truth: not, however, delivered after their manner in a set oration duly ornamented with
words and phrases. No, by heaven! but I shall use the words and
arguments which occur to me at the moment; for I am confident
in the justice of my cause: at my time of life I ought not to be
appearing before you, O men of Athens, in the character of a juve-
nile orator—let no one expect it of me.

And I must beg of you to grant me a favor:—If I defend myself
in my accustomed manner, and you hear me using the words which
I have been in the habit of using in the agora, at the tables of the
money-changers, or anywhere else, I would ask you not to be surprised, and not to interrupt me on this account. For I am more than
seventy years of age, and appearing now for the first time in a court
of law, I am quite a stranger to the language of the place; and therefore I would have you regard me as if I were really a stranger,
whom you would excuse if he spoke in his native tongue, and after
the fashion of his country: Am I making an unfair request of you?
Never mind the manner, which may or may not be good; but think
only of the truth of my words, and give heed to that: let the speaker
speak truly and the judge decide justly.

And first, I have to reply to the older charges and to my first accusers, and then I will go on to the later ones. For of old I have had many accusers, who have accused me falsely to you during many years; and I am more afraid of them than of Anytus and his associates, who are dangerous, too, in their own way. But far more dangerous are the others, who began when you were children, and took possession of your minds with their falsehoods, telling of one Socrates, a wise man, who speculated about the heaven above, and searched into the earth beneath, and made the worse appear the better cause. The disseminators of this tale are the accusers whom I dread; for their hearers are apt to fancy that such enquirers do not believe in the existence of the gods. And they are many, and their charges against me are of ancient date, and they were made by them in the days when you were more impressible than you are now—in childhood, or it may have been in youth—and the cause when heard went by default, for there was none to answer. And hardest of all, I do not know and cannot tell the names of my accusers; unless in the chance case of a Comic poet. All who from envy and malice have persuaded you—some of them having first convinced themselves—all this class of men are most difficult to deal with; for I cannot have them up here, and cross-examine them, and therefore I must simply fight with shadows in my own defense, and argue when there is no one who answers. I will ask you then to assume with me, as I was saying, that my opponents are of two kinds; one recent, the other ancient: and I hope that you will see the propriety of my answering the latter first, for these accusations you heard long before the others, and much oftener.

Well, then, I must make my defense, and endeavor to clear away in a short time a slander which has lasted a long time. May I succeed, if to succeed be for my good and yours, or likely to avail me in my cause! The task is not an easy one; I quite understand the nature of it. And so leaving the event with God, in obedience to the law I will now make my defense.

I will begin at the beginning, and ask what is the accusation which has given rise to the slander of me, and in fact has encouraged Meletus to write out this charge against me. Well, what do the slanderers say? They shall be my prosecutors, and I will sum up their words in an affidavit: "Socrates is an evil-doer, and a curious person, who searches into things under the earth and in heaven, and he makes the worse appear the better cause; and he teaches the aforesaid doctrines to others." Such is the nature of the accusation: it is just what you have yourselves seen in the comedy of Aristophanes [*The Clouds*], who has introduced a man whom he calls Socrates, going about and saying that he walks in air, and talking a deal of nonsense concerning matters of which I do not pretend to know either much or little—not that I mean to speak disparagingly of anyone who is a student of natural philosophy. I should be very sorry if Meletus could bring so grave a charge against me. But the simple truth is, O Athenians, that I have nothing to do with physical speculations. Very many of those here present are witnesses to the truth of this, and to them I appeal. Speak then, you who have heard me, and tell your neighbors whether any of you have ever known me hold forth in few words or in many upon such matters . . . You hear their answer. And from what they say of this part of the charge you will be able to judge of the truth of the rest.

As little foundation is there for the report that I am a teacher, and take money; this accusation has no more truth in it than the other. Although, if a man were really able to instruct mankind, to receive money for giving instruction would, in my opinion, be an honor to him. There is Gorgias of Leontium, and Prodicus of Ceos, and Hippias of Elis, who go the round of the cities, and are able to persuade the young men to leave their own citizens by whom they might be taught for nothing, and come to them whom they not only pay, but are thankful if they may be allowed to pay them. There is at this time a Parian philosopher residing in Athens, of whom I have heard; and I came to hear of him in this way:—I came across a man who has spent a world of money on the Sophists, Callias, the son of Hipponicus, and knowing that he had sons, I asked him: "Callias," I said, "if your two sons were foals or calves, there would be no difficulty in finding someone to put over them; we should hire a trainer of horses, or a farmer probably, who would improve and perfect them in their own proper virtue and excellence; but as they are human beings, whom are you thinking of placing over them? Is there anyone who understands human and political virtue? You must have thought about the matter, for you have sons; is there anyone?" "There is," he said. "Who is he?" said I; "and of what country? And what does he charge?" "Evenus the Parian," he replied; "he is the man, and his charge is five minae." Happy is Evenus, I said to myself, if he really has this wisdom, and teaches at such a moderate charge. Had I the same, I should have been very proud and conceited; but the truth is that I have no knowledge of the kind.

I dare say, Athenians, that someone among you will reply, "Yes, Socrates, but what is the origin of these accusations which are brought against you; there must have been something strange which you have been doing? All these rumors and this talk about you would never have arisen if you had been like other men: tell us, then, what is the cause of them, for we should be sorry to judge hastily of you." Now I regard this as a fair challenge, and I will endeavor to explain to you the reason why I am called wise and have such an evil fame. Please to attend then. And although some of you may think that I am joking, I declare that I will tell you the entire truth.

Men of Athens, this reputation of mine has come of a certain sort of wisdom which I possess. If you ask me what kind of wisdom, I reply, wisdom such as may perhaps be attained by man, for to that extent I am inclined to believe that I am wise; whereas the persons of whom I was speaking have a superhuman wisdom which I may fail to describe, because I have it not myself; and he who says that I have, speaks falsely, and is taking away my character.

And here, O men of Athens, I must beg you not to interrupt me, even if I seem to say something extravagant. For the word which I will speak is not mine. I will refer you to a witness who is worthy of credit; that witness shall be the God of Delphi—he will tell you about my wisdom, if I have any, and of what sort it is. You must have known Chaerephon; he was early a friend of mine, and also a friend of yours, for he shared in the recent exile of the people, and returned with you. Well, Chaerephon, as you know, was very impetuous in all his doings, and he went to Delphi and boldly asked the oracle to tell him whether—as I was saying, I must beg you not to interrupt—he asked the oracle to tell him whether anyone was wiser than I was, and the Pythian prophetess answered, that there was no man wiser. Chaerephon is dead himself; but his brother, who is in court, will confirm the truth of what I am saying.

Why do I mention this? Because I am going to explain to you why I have such an evil name. When I heard the answer, I said to myself, What can the god mean, and what is the interpretation of his riddle? For I know that I have no wisdom, small or great. What then can he mean when he says that I am the wisest of men? And yet he is a god, and cannot lie; that would be against his nature. After long consideration, I thought of a method of trying the question. I reflected that if I could only find a man wiser than myself, then I might go to the god with a refutation in my hand. I should say to him, "Here is a man who is wiser than I am; but you said that I was the wisest." Accordingly I went to one who had the reputation of wisdom, and observed him—his name I need not mention; he was a politician whom I selected for examination—and the result was as follows: When I began to talk with him, I could not help thinking that he was not really wise, although he was thought wise by many, and still wiser by himself; and thereupon I tried to explain to him that he thought himself wise, but was not really wise; and the consequence was that he hated me, and his enmity was shared by several who were present and heard me. So I left him, saying to myself, as I went away: Well, although I do not suppose that either of us knows anything really beautiful and good, I am better off than he is,—for he knows nothing, and thinks that he knows; I neither know nor think that I know. In this latter particular, then, I seem to have slightly the advantage of him. Then I went to another who had still higher pretensions to wisdom, and my conclusion was exactly the same. Whereupon I made another enemy of him, and of many others besides him.

Then I went to one man after another, being not unconscious of the enmity which I provoked, and I lamented and feared this: but necessity was laid upon me,—the word of God, I thought, ought to be considered first. And I said to myself, Go I must to all who appear to know, and find out the meaning of the oracle. And I swear to you, Athenians, by the dog I swear!—for I must tell you the truth—the result of my mission was just this: I found that the men most in repute were all but the most foolish; and that others less esteemed were really wiser and better. I will tell you the tale of my wanderings and of the "Herculean" labors, as I may call them, which I endured only to find at last the oracle irrefutable. After the politicians, I went to the poets; tragic, dithyrambic, and all sorts. And there, I said to myself, you will be instantly detected; now you will find out that you are more ignorant than they are. Accordingly, I took them some of the most elaborate passages in their own writings, and asked what was the meaning of them—thinking that they would teach me something. Will you believe me? I am almost ashamed to confess the truth, but I must say that there is hardly a person present who would not have talked better about their poetry than they did themselves. Then I knew that not by wisdom do poets write poetry, but by a sort of genius and inspiration; they are like diviners or soothsayers who also say many fine things, but do not understand the meaning of them. The poets appeared to me to be much in the same case; and I further observed that upon the strength of their poetry they believed themselves to be the wisest of men in other things in which they were not wise. So I departed, conceiving myself to be superior to them for the same reason that I was superior to the politicians.

At last I went to the artisans. I was conscious that I knew nothing at all, as I may say, and I was sure that they knew many fine things; and here I was not mistaken, for they did know many things of which I was ignorant, and in this they certainly were wiser than I was. But I observed that even the good artisans fell into the same error as the poets;—because they were good workmen they thought that they also knew all sorts of high matters, and this defect in them overshadowed their wisdom; and therefore I asked myself on behalf of the oracle, whether I would like to be as I was, neither having their knowledge nor their ignorance, or like them in both; and I made answer to myself and to the oracle that I was better off as I was.

This inquisition has led to my having many enemies of the worst and most dangerous kind, and has given occasion also to many calumnies. And I am called wise, for my hearers always imagine that I myself possess the wisdom which I find wanting in others: but the truth is, O men of Athens, that God only is wise; and by his answer he intends to show that the wisdom of men is worth little or nothing; he is not speaking of Socrates, he is only using my name by way of illustration, as if he said, "He, O men, is the wisest, who, like Socrates, knows that his wisdom is in truth worth nothing." And so I go about the world, obedient to the god, and search and make enquiry into the wisdom of anyone, whether citizen or stranger, who appears to be wise; and if he is not wise, then in vindication of the oracle I show him that he is not wise; and my occupation quite absorbs me, and I have no time to give either to any public matter of interest or to any concern of my own, but I am in utter poverty by reason of my devotion to the god.

There is another thing:—young men of the richer classes, who have not much to do, come about me of their own accord; they like to hear the pretenders examined, and they often imitate me, and proceed to examine others; there are plenty of persons, as they quickly discover, who think that they know something, but really know little or nothing; and then those who are examined by them instead of being angry with themselves are angry with me: "This confounded Socrates," they say; "this villainous misleader of youth!"—and then if somebody asks them, "Why, what evil does he practice or teach?" they do not know, and cannot tell; but in order that they may not appear to be at a loss, they repeat the ready-made charges which are used against all philosophers about teaching things up in the clouds and under the earth, and having no gods, and making the worse appear the better cause; for they do not like to confess that their pretence of knowledge has been detected—which is the truth; and as they are numerous and ambitious and energetic, and are drawn up in battle array and have persuasive tongues, they have filled your ears with their loud and inveterate calumnies.

And this is the reason why my three accusers, Meletus and Anytus and Lycon, have set upon me; Meletus, who has a quarrel with me on behalf of the poets; Anytus, on behalf of the craftsmen and politicians; Lycon, on behalf of the rhetoricians: and as I said at the beginning, I cannot expect to get rid of such a mass of calumny all in a moment. And this, O men of Athens, is the truth and the whole truth; I have concealed nothing, I have dissembled nothing. And yet, I know that my plainness of speech makes them hate me, and what is their hatred but a proof that I am speaking the truth?— Hence has arisen the prejudice against me; and this is the reason of it, as you will find out either in this or in any future enquiry.

I have said enough in my defense against the first class of my accusers; I turn to the second class. They are headed by Meletus, that good man and true lover of his country, as he calls himself. Against these, too, I must try to make a defense:—Let their affidavit be read: it contains something of this kind: It says that Socrates is a doer of evil, who corrupts the youth; and who does not believe in the gods of the state, but has other new divinities of his own. Such is the charge; and now let us examine the particular counts. He says that I am a doer of evil, and corrupt the youth; but I say, O men of Athens, that Meletus is a doer of evil, in that he pretends to be in earnest when he is only in jest, and is so eager to bring men to trial from a pretended zeal and interest about matters in which he really never had the smallest interest. And the truth of this I will endeavor to prove to you.

Come hither, Meletus, and let me ask a question of you. You think a great deal about the improvement of youth?

Yes, I do.

Tell the judges, then, who is their improver; for you must know, as you have taken the pains to discover their corrupter, and are citing and accusing me before them. Speak, then, and tell the judges who their improver is.—Observe, Meletus, that you are silent, and have nothing to say. But is not this rather disgraceful, and a very considerable proof of what I was saying, that you have no interest in the matter? Speak up, friend, and tell us who their improver is.

The laws.

But that, my good sir, is not my meaning. I want to know who the person is, who, in the first place, knows the laws.

The judges, Socrates, who are present in court.

What, do you mean to say, Meletus, that they are able to instruct and improve youth?

Certainly they are.

What, all of them, or some only and not others?

All of them.

By the goddess Here, that is good news! There are plenty of improvers, then. And what do you say of the audience,—do they improve them?

Yes, they do.

And the senators?

Yes, the senators improve them.

But perhaps the members of the assembly corrupt them?—or do they too improve them?

They improve them.

Then every Athenian improves and elevates them; all with the exception of myself; and I alone am their corrupter? Is that what you affirm?

That is what I stoutly affirm.

I am very unfortunate if you are right. But suppose I ask you a question: How about horses? Does one man do them harm and all the world good? Is not the exact opposite the truth? One man is able to do them good, or at least not many;—the trainer of horses, that is to say, does them good, and others who have to do with them rather injure them? Is not that true, Meletus, of horses, or of any other animals? Most assuredly it is; whether you and Anytus say yes or no. Happy indeed would be the condition of youth if they had one corrupter only, and all the rest of the world were their improvers. But you, Meletus, have sufficiently shown that you never had a thought about the young: your carelessness is seen in your not caring about the very things which you bring against me.

And now, Meletus, I will ask you another question—by Zeus I will: Which is better, to live among bad citizens, or among good ones? Answer, friend, I say; the question is one which may be easily answered. Do not the good do their neighbors good, and the bad do them evil?

Certainly.

And is there anyone who would rather be injured than benefited by those who live with him? Answer, my good friend, the law requires you to answer—does anyone like to be injured?

Certainly not.

And when you accuse me of corrupting and deteriorating the youth, do you allege that I corrupt them intentionally or unintentionally?

Intentionally, I say.

But you have just admitted that the good do their neighbors good, and the evil do them evil. Now, is that a truth which your superior wisdom has recognized thus early in life, and am I, at my age, in such darkness and ignorance as not to know that if a man with whom I have to live is corrupted by me, I am very likely to be harmed by him; and yet I corrupt him, and intentionally, too—so you say, although neither I nor any other human being is ever likely to be convinced by you. But either I do not corrupt them, or I corrupt them unintentionally; and on either view of the case you lie. If my offence is unintentional, the law has no cognizance of unintentional offences: you ought to have taken me privately, and warned and admonished me; for if I had been better advised, I should have left off doing what I only did unintentionally—no doubt I should; but you would have nothing to say to me and refused to teach me. And now you bring me up in this court, which is a place not of instruction, but of punishment.

It will be very clear to you, Athenians, as I was saying, that Meletus has no care at all, great or small, about the matter. But still I should like to know, Meletus, in what I am affirmed to corrupt the young. I suppose you mean, as I infer from your indictment, that I teach them not to acknowledge the gods which the state acknowledges, but some other new divinities or spiritual agencies in their stead. These are the lessons by which I corrupt the youth, as you say.

Yes, that I say emphatically.

Then, by the gods, Meletus, of whom we are speaking, tell me and the court, in somewhat plainer terms, what you mean! For I do not as yet understand whether you affirm that I teach other men to acknowledge some gods, and therefore that I do believe in gods, and am not an entire atheist—this you do not lay to my charge,—but only you say that they are not the same gods which the city recognizes—the charge is that they are different gods. Or, do you mean that I am an atheist simply, and a teacher of atheism?

I mean the latter—that you are a complete atheist.

What an extraordinary statement! Why do you think so, Meletus? Do you mean that I do not believe in the godhead of the sun or moon, like other men?

I assure you, judges, that he does not: for he says that the sun is stone, and the moon earth.

Friend Meletus, you think that you are accusing Anaxagoras: and you have but a bad opinion of the judges, if you fancy them illiterate to such a degree as not to know that these doctrines are found in the books of Anaxagoras the Clazomenian, which are full of them. And so, forsooth, the youth are said to be taught them by Socrates, when there are not unfrequently exhibitions of them at the theater (price of admission, one drachma at the most); and they might pay their money, and laugh at Socrates if he pretends to father these extraordinary views. And so, Meletus, you really think that I do not believe in any god?

I swear by Zeus that you believe absolutely in none at all.

Nobody will believe you, Meletus, and I am pretty sure that you do not believe yourself. I cannot help thinking, men of Athens, that Meletus is reckless and impudent, and that he has written this indictment in a spirit of mere wantonness and youthful bravado. Has he not compounded a riddle, thinking to try me? He said to himself:—I shall see whether the wise Socrates will discover my facetious contradiction, or whether I shall be able to deceive him and the rest of them. For he certainly does appear to me to contradict himself in the indictment as much as if he said that Socrates is guilty of not believing in the gods, and yet of believing in them—but this is not like a person who is in earnest.

I should like you, O men of Athens, to join me in examining what I conceive to be his inconsistency; and do you, Meletus, answer. And I must remind the audience of my request that they would not make a disturbance if I speak in my accustomed manner:

Did ever man, Meletus, believe in the existence of human things, and not of human beings? . . . I wish, men of Athens, that he would answer, and not be always trying to get up an interruption. Did ever any man believe in horsemanship, and not in horses, or in flute-playing, and not in flute-players? No, my friend; I will answer to you and to the court, as you refuse to answer for yourself. There is no man who ever did. But now please to answer the next question: Can a man believe in spiritual and divine agencies, and not in spirits or demigods?

He cannot.

How lucky I am to have extracted that answer, by the assistance of the court! But then you swear in the indictment that I teach and believe in divine or spiritual agencies (new or old, no matter for that); at any rate, I believe in spiritual agencies,—so you say and swear in the affidavit; and yet if I believe in divine beings, how can I help believing in spirits or demigods;—must I not? To be sure I must; and therefore I may assume that your silence gives consent. Now what are spirits or demigods? Are they not either gods or the sons of gods?

Certainly they are.

But this is what I call the facetious riddle invented by you: the demigods or spirits are gods, and you say first that I do not believe in gods, and then again that I do believe in gods; that is, if I believe in demigods. For if the demigods are the illegitimate sons of gods, whether by the nymphs or by any other mothers, of whom they are said to be the sons—what human being will ever believe that there are no gods if they are the sons of gods? You might as well affirm the existence of mules, and deny that of horses and asses. Such nonsense, Meletus, could only have been intended by you to make trial of me. You have put this into the indictment because you had nothing real of which to accuse me. But no one who has a particle of understanding will ever be convinced by you that the same men can believe in divine and superhuman things, and yet not believe that there are gods and demigods and heroes.

I have said enough in answer to the charge of Meletus: any elaborate defense is unnecessary, but I know only too well how many are the enmities which I have incurred, and this is what will be my destruction if I am destroyed;—not Meletus, nor yet Anytus, but the envy and detraction of the world, which has been the death of many good men, and will probably be the death of many more; there is no danger of my being the last of them.

Someone will say: And are you not ashamed, Socrates, of a course of life which is likely to bring you to an untimely end? To him I may fairly answer: There you are mistaken: a man who is good for anything ought not to calculate the chance of living or dying; he ought only to consider whether in doing anything he is doing right or wrong—acting the part of a good man or of a bad. Whereas, upon your view, the heroes who fell at Troy were not good for much, and the son of Thetis above all, who altogether despised danger in comparison with disgrace; and when he was so eager to slay Hector, his goddess mother said to him, that if he avenged his companion Patroclus, and slew Hector, he would die himself—"Fate," she said, in these or the like words, "waits for you next after Hector"; he, receiving this warning, utterly despised danger and death, and instead of fearing them, feared rather to live in dishonor, and not to avenge his friend. "Let me die forthwith," he replies, "and be avenged of my enemy, rather than abide here by the beaked ships, a laughing-stock and a burden of the earth." Had Achilles any thought of death and danger? For wherever a man's place is, whether the place which he has chosen or that in which he has been placed by a commander, there he ought to remain in the hour of danger; he should not think of death or of anything but of disgrace. And this, O men of Athens, is a true saying.

Strange, indeed, would be my conduct, O men of Athens, if I who, when I was ordered by the generals whom you chose to command me at Potidaea and Amphipolis and Delium, remained where they placed me, like any other man, facing death—if now, when, as I conceive and imagine, God orders me to fulfil the philosopher's mission of searching into myself and other men, I were to desert my post through fear of death, or any other fear; that would indeed be strange, and I might justly be arraigned in court for denying the existence of the gods, if I disobeyed the oracle because I was afraid of death, fancying that I was wise when I was not wise. For the fear of death is indeed the pretence of wisdom, and not real wisdom, being a pretence of knowing the unknown; and no one knows whether death, which men in their fear apprehend to be the great-est evil, may not be the greatest good. Is not this ignorance of a disgraceful sort, the ignorance which is the conceit that a man knows what he does not know? And in this respect only I believe myself to differ from men in general, and may perhaps claim to be wiser than they are:—that whereas I know but little of the world below, I do not suppose that I know: but I do know that injustice and disobedience to a better, whether God or man, is evil and dis-honorable, and I will never fear or avoid a possible good rather than a certain evil.

And therefore if you let me go now, and are not convinced by Anytus, who said that since I had been prosecuted I must be put to death; (or if not that I ought never to have been prosecuted at all); and that if I escape now, your sons will all be utterly ruined by listening to my words—if you say to me, "Socrates, this time we will not mind Anytus, and you shall be let off, but upon one condi-tion, that you are not to enquire and speculate in this way any more, and that if you are caught doing so again you shall die";—if this was the condition on which you let me go, I should reply: "Men of Athens, I honor and love you; but I shall obey God rather than you, and while I have life and strength I shall never cease from the practice and teaching of philosophy, exhorting anyone whom I meet and saying to him after my manner: You, my friend,—a citi-zen of the great and mighty and wise city of Athens,—are you not ashamed of heaping up the greatest amount of money and honor and reputation, and caring so little about wisdom and truth and the greatest improvement of the soul, which you never regard or heed at all?" And if the person with whom I am arguing, says: "Yes, but I do care"; then I do not leave him or let him go at once; but I proceed to interrogate and examine and cross-examine him, and if I think that he has no virtue in him, but only says that he has, I reproach him with undervaluing the greater, and overvaluing the less. And I shall repeat the same words to everyone whom I meet, young and old, citizen and alien, but especially to the citizens, inas-much as they are my brethren.

For know that this is the command of God; and I believe that no greater good has ever happened in the state than my service to the God. For I do nothing but go about persuading you all, old and young alike, not to take thought for your persons or your proper-ties, but first and chiefly to care about the greatest improvement of the soul. I tell you that virtue is not given by money, but that from virtue comes money and every other good of man, public as well as private. This is my teaching, and if this is the doctrine which corrupts the youth, I am a mischievous person. But if anyone says that this is not my teaching, he is speaking an untruth. Wherefore, O men of Athens, I say to you, do as Anytus bids or not as Anytus bids, and either acquit me or not; but whichever you do, understand that I shall never alter my ways, not even if I have to die many times.

Men of Athens, do not interrupt, but hear me; there was an understanding between us that you should hear me to the end: I have something more to say, at which you may be inclined to cry out; but I believe that to hear me will be good for you, and therefore I beg that you will not cry out. I would have you know, that if you kill such a one as I am, you will injure yourselves more than you will injure me. Nothing will injure me, not Meletus nor yet Anytus—they cannot, for a bad man is not permitted to injure a better than himself. I do not deny that Anytus may, perhaps, kill him, or drive him into exile, or deprive him of civil rights; and he may imagine, and others may imagine, that he is inflicting a great injury upon him: but there I do not agree. For the evil of doing as he is doing—the evil of unjustly taking away the life of another—is greater far.

And now, Athenians, I am not going to argue for my own sake, as you may think, but for yours, that you may not sin against the God by condemning me, who am his gift to you. For if you kill me you will not easily find a successor to me, who, if I may use such a ludicrous figure of speech, am a sort of gadfly, given to the state by God; and the state is a great and noble steed who is tardy in his motions owing to his very size, and requires to be stirred into life. I am that gadfly which God has attached to the state, and all day long and in all places am always fastening upon you, arousing and persuading and reproaching you. You will not easily find another like me, and therefore I would advise you to spare me. I dare say that you may feel out of temper (like a person who is suddenly awakened from sleep), and you think that you might easily strike me dead as Anytus advises, and then you would sleep on for the remainder of your lives, unless God in his care of you sent you another gadfly.

When I say that I am given to you by God, the proof of my mission is this:—if I had been like other men, I should not have neglected all my own concerns or patiently seen the neglect of them during all these years, and have been doing yours, coming to you individually like a father or elder brother, exhorting you to regard virtue; such conduct, I say, would be unlike human nature. If I had gained anything, or if my exhortations had been paid, there would have been some sense in my doing so; but now, as you will perceive, not even the impudence of my accusers dares to say that I have ever exacted or sought pay of anyone; of that they have no witness. And I have a sufficient witness to the truth of what I say—my poverty.

Someone may wonder why I go about in private giving advice and busying myself with the concerns of others, but do not venture to come forward in public and advise the state. I will tell you why. You have heard me speak at sundry times and in divers places of an oracle or sign which comes to me, and is the divinity which Meletus ridicules in the indictment. This sign, which is a kind of voice, first began to come to me when I was a child; it always forbids but never commands me to do anything which I am going to do. This is what deters me from being a politician. And rightly, as I think. For I am certain, O men of Athens, that if I had engaged in politics, I should have perished long ago, and done no good either to you or to myself. And do not be offended at my telling you the truth: for the truth is, that no man who goes to war with you or any other multitude, honestly striving against the many lawless and unrighteous deeds which are done in a state, will save his life; he who will fight for the right, if he would live even for a brief space, must have a private station and not a public one.

I can give you convincing evidence of what I say, not words only, but what you value far more—actions. Let me relate to you a passage of my own life which will prove to you that I should never have yielded to injustice from any fear of death, and that "as I should have refused to yield" I must have died at once. I will tell you a tale of the courts, not very interesting perhaps, but nevertheless true. The only office of state which I ever held, O men of Athens, was that of senator: the tribe Antiochis, which is my tribe, had the presidency at the trial of the generals who had not taken up the bodies of the slain after the battle of Arginusae; and you proposed to try them in a body, contrary to law, as you all thought afterwards; but at the time I was the only one of the Prytanes who was opposed to the illegality, and I gave my vote against you; and when the orators threatened to impeach and arrest me, and you called and shouted, I made up my mind that I would run the risk, having law and justice with me, rather than take part in your injustice because I feared imprisonment and death. This happened in the days of the democracy. But when the oligarchy of the Thirty was in power, they sent for me and four others into the rotunda, and bade us bring Leon the Salaminian from Salamis, as they wanted to put him to death. This was a specimen of the sort of commands which they were always giving with the view of implicating as many as possible in their crimes; and then I showed, not in word only but in deed, that, if I may be allowed to use such an expression, I cared not a straw for death, and that my great and only care was lest I should do an unrighteous or unholy thing. For the strong arm of that oppressive power did not frighten me into doing wrong; and when we came out of the rotunda the other four went to Salamis and fetched Leon, but I went quietly home. For which I might have lost my life, had not the power of the Thirty shortly afterwards come to an end. And many will witness to my words.

Now do you really imagine that I could have survived all these years, if I had led a public life, supposing that like a good man I had always maintained the right and had made justice, as I ought, the first thing? No indeed, men of Athens, neither I nor any other man. But I have been always the same in all my actions, public as well as private, and never have I yielded any base compliance to those who are slanderously termed my disciples, or to any other. Not that I have any regular disciples. But if anyone likes to come and hear me while I am pursuing my mission, whether he be young or old, he is not excluded. Nor do I converse only with those who pay; but anyone, whether he be rich or poor, may ask and answer me and listen to my words; and whether he turns out to be a bad man or a good one, neither result can be justly imputed to me; for I never taught or professed to teach him anything. And if anyone says that he has ever learned or heard anything from me in private which all the world has not heard, let me tell you that he is lying.

But I shall be asked, Why do people delight in continually conversing with you? I have told you already, Athenians, the whole truth about this matter: they like to hear the cross-examination of the pretenders to wisdom; there is amusement in it. Now this duty of cross-examining other men has been imposed upon me by God; and has been signified to me by oracles, visions, and in every way in which the will of divine power was ever intimated to anyone.

This is true, O Athenians, or, if not true, would be soon refuted. If I am or have been corrupting the youth, those of them who are now grown up and have become sensible that I gave them bad advice in the days of their youth should come forward as accusers, and take their revenge; or if they do not like to come themselves, some of their relatives, fathers, brothers, or other kinsmen, should say what evil their families have suffered at my hands. Now is their time. Many of them I see in the court. There is Crito, who is of the same age and of the same deme with myself, and there is Critobulus his son, whom I also see. Then again there is Lysanias of Sphettus, who is the father of Aeschines—he is present; and also there is Antiphon of Cephisus, who is the father of Epigenes; and there are the brothers of several who have associated with me. There is Nicostratus the son of Theosdotides, and the brother of Theodotus (now Theodotus himself is dead, and therefore he, at any rate, will not seek to stop him); and there is Paralus the son of Demodocus, who had a brother Theages; and Adeimantus the son of Ariston, whose brother Plato is present; and Aeantodorus, who is the brother of Apollodorus, whom I also see. I might mention a great many others, some of whom Meletus should have produced as witnesses in the course of his speech; and let him still produce them, if he has forgotten—I will make way for him. And let him say, if he has any testimony of the sort which he can produce. Nay, Athenians, the very opposite is the truth. For all these are ready to witness on behalf of the corrupter, of the injurer of their kindred, as Meletus and Anytus call me; not the corrupted youth only— there might have been a motive for that—but their uncorrupted elder relatives. Why should they too support me with their testimony? Why, indeed, except for the sake of truth and justice, and because they know that I am speaking the truth, and that Meletus is a liar.

Well, Athenians, this and the like of this is all the defense which I have to offer. Yet a word more. Perhaps there may be someone who is offended at me, when he calls to mind how he himself on a similar, or even a less serious occasion, prayed and entreated the judges with many tears, and how he produced his children in court, which was a moving spectacle, together with a host of relations and friends; whereas I, who am probably in danger of my life, will do none of these things. The contrast may occur to his mind, and he may be set against me, and vote in anger because he is displeased at me on this account. Now if there be such a person among you,— mind, I do not say that there is,—to him I may fairly reply:

My friend, I am a man, and like other men, a creature of flesh and blood, and not "of wood or stone," as Homer says; and I have a family, yes, and sons, O Athenians, three in number, one almost a man, and two others who are still young; and yet I will not bring any of them hither in order to petition you for an acquittal. And why not? Not from any self-assertion or want of respect for you. Whether I am or am not afraid of death is another question, of which I will not now speak. But, having regard to public opinion, I feel that such conduct would be discreditable to myself, and to you, and to the whole state. One who has reached my years, and who has a name for wisdom, ought not to demean himself. Whether this opinion of me be deserved or not, at any rate the world has decided that Socrates is in some way superior to other men. And if those among you who are said to be superior in wisdom and courage, and any other virtue, demean themselves in this way, how shameful is their conduct! I have seen men of reputation, when they have been condemned, behaving in the strangest manner: they seemed to fancy that they were going to suffer something dreadful if they died, and that they could be immortal if you only allowed them to live; and I think that such are a dishonor to the state, and that any stranger coming in would have said of them that the most eminent men of Athens, to whom the Athenians themselves give honor and command, are no better than women. And I say that these things ought not to be done by those of us who have a reputation; and if they are done, you ought not to permit them; you ought rather to show that you are far more disposed to condemn the man who gets up a doleful scene and makes the city ridiculous, than him who holds his peace.

But, setting aside the question of public opinion, there seems to be something wrong in asking a favor of a judge, and thus procuring an acquittal, instead of informing and convincing him. For his duty is, not to make a present of justice, but to give judgment; and he has sworn that he will judge according to the laws, and not according to his own good pleasure; and we ought not to encourage you, nor should you allow yourselves to be encouraged, in this habit of perjury—there can be no piety in that. Do not then require me to do what I consider dishonorable and impious and wrong, especially now, when I am being tried for impiety on the

indictment of Meletus. For if, O men of Athens, by force of persuasion and entreaty I could overpower your oaths, then I should be
teaching you to believe that there are no gods, and in defending
should simply convict myself of the charge of not believing in
them. But that is not so—far otherwise. For I do believe that there
are gods, and in a sense higher than that in which any of my accusers believe in them. And to you and to God I commit my cause, to
be determined by you as is best for you and me.

*[The jury then declared Socrates guilty; Meletus called for the death
penalty.]*

There are many reasons why I am not grieved, O men of Athens,
at the vote of condemnation. I expected it, and am only surprised
that the votes are so nearly equal; for I had thought that the majority
against me would have been far larger; but now, had thirty votes
gone over to the other side, I should have been acquitted. And I
may say, I think, that I have escaped Meletus. I may say more; for
without the assistance of Anytus and Lycon, anyone may see that he
would not have had a fifth part of the votes, as the law requires, in
which case he would have incurred a fine of a thousand drachmae.

And so he proposes death as the penalty. And what shall I propose on my part, O men of Athens? Clearly that which is my due.
And what is my due? What return shall be made to the man who
has never had the wit to be idle during his whole life; but has been
careless of what the many care for—wealth, and family interests,
and military offices, and speaking in the assembly, and magistracies,
and plots, and parties. Reflecting that I was really too honest a man
to be a politician and live, I did not go where I could do no good
to you or to myself; but where I could do the greatest good privately to every one of you, thither I went, and sought to persuade
every man among you that he must look to himself, and seek virtue
and wisdom before he looks to his private interests, and look to the
state before he looks to the interests of the state; and that this should
be the order which he observes in all his actions.

What shall be done to such a one? Doubtless some good thing,
O men of Athens, if he has his reward; and the good should be of
a kind suitable to him. What would be a reward suitable to a poor
man who is your benefactor, and who desires leisure that he may
instruct you? There can be no reward so fitting as maintenance in

the Prytaneum, O men of Athens, a reward which he deserves far
more than the citizen who has won the prize at Olympia in the
horse or chariot race, whether the chariots were drawn by two
horses or by many. For I am in want, and he has enough; and he
only gives you the appearance of happiness, and I give you the reality. And if I am to estimate the penalty fairly, I should say that
maintenance in the Prytaneum is the just return.

Perhaps you think that I am braving you in what I am saying
now, as in what I said before about the tears and prayers. But this is
not so. I speak rather because I am convinced that I never intentionally wronged anyone, although I cannot convince you—the time
has been too short; if there were a law at Athens, as there is in other
cities, that a capital cause should not be decided in one day, then I
believe that I should have convinced you. But I cannot in a moment
refute great slanders; and, as I am convinced that I never wronged
another, I will assuredly not wrong myself. I will not say of myself
that I deserve any evil, or propose any penalty. Why should I?
Because I am afraid of the penalty of death which Meletus proposes?
When I do not know whether death is a good or an evil, why
should I propose a penalty which would certainly be an evil? Shall
I say imprisonment? And why should I live in prison, and be the
slave of the magistrates of the year—of the Eleven? Or shall the
penalty be a fine, and imprisonment until the fine is paid? There is
the same objection. I should have to lie in prison, for money I have
none, and cannot pay. And if I say exile (and this may possibly be
the penalty which you will affix), I must indeed be blinded by the
love of life, if I am so irrational as to expect that when you, who are
my own citizens, cannot endure my discourses and words, and have
found them so grievous and odious that you will have no more of
them, others are likely to endure me. No indeed, men of Athens,
that is not very likely. And what a life should I lead, at my age,
wandering from city to city, ever changing my place of exile, and
always being driven out! For I am quite sure that wherever I go,
there, as here, the young men will flock to me; and if I drive them
away, their elders will drive me out at their request; and if I let them
come, their fathers and friends will drive me out for their sakes.

Someone will say: "Yes, Socrates, but cannot you hold your
tongue? And then you may go into a foreign city, and no one will
interfere with you." Now I have great difficulty in making you
understand my answer to this. For if I tell you that to do as you say

would be a disobedience to the god, and therefore that I cannot hold my tongue, you will not believe that I am serious; and if I say again that daily to discourse about virtue, and of those other things about which you hear me examining myself and others, is the greatest good of man, and that the unexamined life is not worth living, you are still less likely to believe me. Yet I say what is true, although a thing of which it is hard for me to persuade you. Also, I have never been accustomed to think that I deserve to suffer any harm. Had I money I might have estimated the offence at what I was able to pay, and not have been much the worse. But I have none, and therefore I must ask you to proportion the fine to my means. Well, perhaps I could afford a mina, and therefore I propose that penalty: Plato, Crito, Critobulus, and Apollodorus, my friends here, bid me say thirty minae, and they will be the sureties. Let thirty minae be the penalty; for which sum they will be ample security to you.

[The jury then voted for the death penalty.]

Not much time will be gained, O Athenians, in return for the evil name which you will get from the detractors of the city, who will say that you killed Socrates, a wise man; for they will call me wise, even although I am not wise, when they want to reproach you. If you had waited a little while, your desire would have been fulfilled in the course of nature. For I am far advanced in years, as you may perceive, and not far from death. I am speaking now not to all of you, but only to those who have condemned me to death. And I have another thing to say to them: you think that I was convicted because I had no words of the sort which would have procured my acquittal—I mean, if I had thought fit to leave nothing undone or unsaid. Not so; the deficiency which led to my conviction was not of words—certainly not. But I had not the boldness or impudence or inclination to address you as you would have liked me to do, weeping and wailing and lamenting, and saying and doing many things which you have been accustomed to hear from others, and which, as I maintain, are unworthy of me. I thought at the time that I ought not to do anything common or mean when in danger: nor do I now repent of the style of my defense; I would rather die having spoken after my manner, than speak in your manner and live. For neither in war nor yet at law ought I or any man to use every way of escaping death. Often in battle there can be no doubt that if a man will throw away his arms, and fall on his knees before his pursuers, he may escape death; and in other dangers there are other ways of escaping death, if a man is willing to say and do anything. The difficulty, my friends, is not to avoid death, but to avoid unrighteousness; for that runs faster than death.

I am old and move slowly, and the slower runner has overtaken me, and my accusers are keen and quick, and the faster runner, who is unrighteousness, has overtaken them. And now I depart hence condemned by you to suffer the penalty of death,—they too go their ways condemned by the truth to suffer the penalty of villainy and wrong; and I must abide by my award—let them abide by theirs. I suppose that these things may be regarded as fated,—and I think that they are well.

And now, O men who have condemned me, I would fain prophesy to you; for I am about to die, and in the hour of death men are gifted with prophetic power. And I prophesy to you who are my murderers, that immediately after my departure punishment far heavier than you have inflicted on me will surely await you. Me you have killed because you wanted to escape the accuser, and not to give an account of your lives. But that will not be as you suppose: far otherwise. For I say that there will be more accusers of you than there are now; accusers whom hitherto I have restrained: and as they are younger they will be more inconsiderate with you, and you will be more offended at them. If you think that by killing men you can prevent someone from censuring your evil lives, you are mistaken; that is not a way of escape which is either possible or honorable; the easiest and the noblest way is not to be disabling others, but to be improving yourselves. This is the prophecy which I utter before my departure to the judges who have condemned me.

Friends, who would have acquitted me, I would like also to talk with you about the thing which has come to pass, while the magistrates are busy, and before I go to the place at which I must die. Stay then a little, for we may as well talk with one another while there is time. You are my friends, and I should like to show you the meaning of this event which has happened to me. O my judges—for you I may truly call judges—I should like to tell you of a wonderful circumstance. Hitherto the divine faculty of which the internal oracle is the source has constantly been in the habit of opposing me even about trifles, if I was going to make a slip or error in any matter; and now as you see there has come upon me that which may be thought, and is generally believed to be, the last and worst evil. But the oracle made no sign of opposition, either when I was leaving my house in the morning, or when I was on my way to the court, or while I was speaking, at anything which I was going to say; and yet I have often been stopped in the middle of a speech, but now in nothing I either said or did touching the matter in hand has the oracle opposed me. What do I take to be the explanation of this silence? I will tell you. It is an intimation that what has happened to me is a good, and that those of us who think that death is an evil are in error. For the customary sign would surely have opposed me had I been going to evil and not to good.

Let us reflect in another way, and we shall see that there is great reason to hope that death is a good; for one of two things—either death is a state of nothingness and utter unconsciousness, or, as men say, there is a change and migration of the soul from this world to another. Now if you suppose that there is no consciousness, but a sleep like the sleep of him who is undisturbed even by dreams, death will be an unspeakable gain. For if a person were to select the night in which his sleep was undisturbed even by dreams, and were to compare with this the other days and nights of his life, and then were to tell us how many days and nights he had passed in the course of his life better and more pleasantly than this one, I think that any man, I will not say a private man, but even the great king will not find many such days or nights, when compared with the others. Now if death be of such a nature, I say that to die is gain; for eternity is then only a single night. But if death is the journey to another place, and there, as men say, all the dead abide, what good, O my friends and judges, can be greater than this? If indeed when the pilgrim arrives in the world below, he is delivered from the professors of justice in this world, and finds the true judges who are said to give judgment there, Minos and Rhadamanthus and Aeacus and Triptolemus, and other sons of God who were righteous in their own life, that pilgrimage will be worth making. What would not a man give if he might converse with Orpheus and Musaeus and Hesiod and Homer? Nay, if this be true, let me die again and again. I myself, too, shall have a wonderful interest in there meeting and conversing with Palamedes, and Ajax the son of Telamon, and any other ancient hero who has suffered death through an unjust judgment; and there will be no small pleasure, as I think, in comparing my own sufferings with theirs.

Above all, I shall then be able to continue my search into true and false knowledge; as in this world, so also in the next; and I shall find out who is wise, and who pretends to be wise, and is not. What would not a man give, O judges, to be able to examine the leader of the great Trojan expedition; or Odysseus or Sisyphus, or numberless others, men and women too! What infinite delight would there be in conversing with them and asking them questions! In another world they do not put a man to death for asking questions: assuredly not. For besides being happier than we are, they will be immortal, if what is said is true.

Wherefore, O judges, be of good cheer about death, and know of a certainty, that no evil can happen to a good man, either in life or after death. He and his are not neglected by the gods; nor has my own approaching end happened by mere chance. But I see clearly that the time had arrived when it was better for me to die and be released from trouble; wherefore the oracle gave no sign. For which reason, also, I am not angry with my condemners, or with my accusers; they have done me no harm, although they did not mean to do me any good; and for this I may gently blame them.

Still I have a favor to ask of them. When my sons are grown up, I would ask you, O my friends, to punish them; and I would have you trouble them, as I have troubled you, if they seem to care about riches, or anything, more than about virtue; or if they pretend to be something when they are really nothing,—then reprove them, as I have reproved you, for not caring about that for which they ought to care, and thinking that they are something when they are really nothing. And if you do this, both I and my sons will have received justice at your hands.

The hour of departure has arrived, and we go our ways—I to die, and you to live. Which is better God only knows.

SOURCE: Benjamin Jowett. *The Dialogues of Plato: Translated into English, with Analyses and Introductions*. Volume 2. New York: Scribner, Armstrong and Company. 1874.

DEMOSTHENES

THE FIRST PHILIPPIC (351 B.C.)

Demosthenes (c. 383–322 B.C.) is the most renowned of the ten
"Attic Orators" (at least in part because most of the work of the
other nine has disappeared). Demosthenes apparently "did publish
speeches in his lifetime, perhaps to substantiate their political
importance."[1] He was not a natural speaker, the historian Plutarch
tells us, but "to make himself a master in rhetoric, applied all the
faculties he had, natural or acquired, wholly that way that he far
surpassed in force and strength of eloquence all his contemporaries
in political and judicial speaking, in grandeur and majesty all the
panegyrical orators, and in accuracy and science all the logicians and
rhetoricians of his day . . ." Plutarch compared him to the Roman
orator Cicero and preferred the Greek statesman: "For Demosthenes's
oratory was without all embellishment and jesting, wholly composed for real effect and seriousness; not smelling of the lamp . . .
but of the temperance, thoughtfulness, austerity, and grave earnest-
ness of his temper."[2] In the following speech he attempts to rouse
Athens' suspicion of the Macedonian King Philip II.

Had we been convened, Athenians, on some new subject of debate,
I had waited until most of the usual persons had declared their
opinions. If I had approved of anything proposed by them, I should

---

[1]A. N. W. Saunders. *Greek Political Oratory*. Harmondsworth, England: Penguin.
1970. 13.
[2]*The Lives of the Nobel Grecians and Romans*. Translated by John Dryden. Revised
by Arthur Hugh Clough. New York: Modern Library (Random House). 1932.

have continued silent; if not, I had then attempted to speak my sentiments. But since those very points on which these speakers have often been heard already are, at this time, to be considered, though I have risen first, I presume I may expect your pardon; for if they on former occasions had advised the necessary measures, you would not have found it needful to consult at present.

First, then, Athenians, these our affairs must not be thought desperate: no, though their situation seems entirely deplorable; for the most shocking circumstance of all our past conduct is really the most favorable to our future expectations. And what is this? That our own total indolence has been the cause of all our present difficulties: for were we thus distressed, in spite of every vigorous effort which the honor of our State demanded, there were then no hope of a recovery.

In the next place, reflect—you who have been informed by others, and you who can yourselves remember—how great a power the Lacedaemonians not long since possessed; and with what resolution, with what dignity you disdained to act unworthy of the State, but maintained the war against them for the rights of Greece. Why do I mention these things? That you may know, that you may see, Athenians, that if duly vigilant you cannot have anything to fear; that if once remiss, not anything can happen agreeably to your desires: witness the then powerful arms of Lacedaemon, which a just attention to your interests enabled you to vanquish; and this man's late insolent attempt, which our insensibility to all our great concerns has made the cause of this confusion.

If there be a man in this assembly who thinks that we must find a formidable enemy in Philip, while he views, on one hand, the numerous armies which attend him, and, on the other, the weakness of the State thus despoiled of its dominions—he thinks justly. Yet let him reflect on this: there was a time, Athenians, when we possessed Pydna, and Potidaea, and Methone, and all that country round; when many of those States now subjected to him were free and independent, and more inclined to our alliance than to his. Had then Philip reasoned in the same manner, "How shall I dare to attack the Athenians, whose garrisons command my territory, while I am destitute of all assistance?" he would not have engaged in those enterprises which are now crowned with success; nor could he have raised himself to this pitch of greatness. No, Athenians, he knew this well, that all these places are but prizes, laid between the combatants, and ready for the conqueror: that the dominions of the absent devolve naturally to those who are in the field; the possessions of the supine to the active and intrepid. Animated by these sentiments, he overturns whole countries; he holds all people in subjection: some, as by the right of conquest; others, under the titles of allies and confederates; for all are willing to confederate with those whom they see prepared and resolved to exert themselves as they ought.

And if you, my countrymen, will now at length be persuaded to entertain the like sentiments; if each of you, renouncing all evasions, will be ready to approve himself a useful citizen, to the utmost that his station and abilities demand; if the rich will be ready to contribute, and the young to take the field; in one word, if you will be yourselves, and banish those vain hopes which every single person entertains, that while so many others are engaged in public business, his service will not be required; you then (if Heaven so pleases) shall regain your dominions, recall those opportunities your supineness has neglected, and chastise the insolence of this man; for you are not to imagine that, like a god, he is to enjoy his present greatness forever fixed and unchangeable. No, Athenians, there are those who hate him, who fear him, who envy him, even among those seemingly the most attached to his cause. These are passions common to mankind; nor must we think that his friends only are exempted from them. It is true they lie concealed at present, as our indolence deprives them of all resource.

But let us shake off this indolence; for you see how we are situated; you see the outrageous arrogance of this man, who does not leave it to your choice whether you shall act or remain quiet; but braves you with his menaces; and talks, as we are informed, in a strain of the highest extravagance; and is not able to rest satisfied with his present acquisitions, but is even in pursuit of further conquests; and while we sit down, inactive and irresolute, encloses us on all sides with his toils. When, therefore, O my countrymen! when will you exert your vigor? When roused by some event? When forced by some necessity? What then are we to think of our present condition? To freemen, the disgrace attending on misconduct is, in my opinion, the most urgent necessity. Or say, is it your sole ambition to wander through the public places, each inquiring of the other, "What new advice?" Can anything be more new than that a man of Macedon should conquer the Athenians and give law to Greece? "Is Philip dead?" "No, but in great danger." How are you concerned in those rumors? Suppose he should meet some fatal stroke; you would soon raise up another Philip, if your interests are thus regarded; for it is not to his own strength that he so much owes his elevation as to our supineness. And should some accident affect him, should Fortune, who has ever been more careful of the State than we ourselves, now repeat her favors (and may she thus crown them!); be assured of this, that by being on the spot, ready to take advantage of the confusion, you will everywhere be absolute masters; but in your present disposition, even if a favorable juncture should present you with Amphipolis, you could not take possession of it while this suspense prevails in your designs and in your councils.

And now, as to the necessity of a general vigor and alacrity; of this you must be fully persuaded; this point, therefore, I shall urge no further. But the nature of the armament which, I think, will extricate you from the present difficulties, the numbers to be raised, the subsidies required for their support, and all the other necessaries; how they may (in my opinion) be best and most expeditiously provided; these things I shall endeavor to explain. But here I make this request, Athenians—that you would not be precipitate, but suspend your judgment till you have heard me fully. And if, at first, I seem to propose a new kind of armament, let it not be thought that I am delaying your affairs; for it is not they who cry out, "Instantly!" "This moment!" whose counsels suit the present juncture (as it is not possible to repel violences already committed by any occasional detachment); but he who will show you of what kind that armament must be, how great, and how supported, which may subsist until we yield to peace, or until our enemies sink beneath our arms; for thus only can we be secured from future dangers. These things, I think, I can point out; not that I would prevent any other person from declaring his opinion. Thus far am I engaged; how I can acquit myself will immediately appear; to your judgments I appeal.

SOURCE: *All the Orations of Demosthenes: Pronounced to Excite the Athenians Against Philip, King of Macedon.* Translated by Thomas Leland. London: W. Johnston. 1757.

HEGESIPPUS

ON THE HALONNESUS (342 B.C.)

Hegesippus, about whom little is known beyond this speech (which has occasionally been assigned to Demonsthenes' authorship), was a compatriot of Demosthenes who in 343 traveled to King Philip II of Macedonia to negotiate for Athens the return of its island Halonnesus. Rebuffed, Hegesippus returned home; the next year, Philip decided to offer the island to Athens, after all. In the ensuing debate in the Athenian assembly, Hegesippus argues against accepting Philip's terms.

Men of Athens! It is by no means reasonable that the complaints which Philip urges against those speakers who assert your rights should deprive us of the liberty of enforcing the true interests of our country. Grievous, indeed, would be the case if the freedom of our public debates were to be at once destroyed by a letter sent from him. It is my present purpose, first, to examine the several allegations mentioned in this letter; then shall we proceed to the other particulars urged by his ambassadors.

Philip begins with speaking of the Halonnesus: this island, he declares, is his; that he presents it to us as a free gift; that we have no rightful claims to it; nor has he injured our property either in acquiring or in keeping possession of it. Such were his professions at the time when we were sent on our embassy to Macedon: that he had won this island from the pirates who had seized it, and was therefore justified in keeping his acquisition. But, as this plea has no support from truth and justice, it is not difficult to deprive him of it. The places seized by pirates are ever the property of some others; these they fortify, and from thence make their excursions. But the man who punishes their outrages, and drives them out, cannot reasonably allege that the possessions which these pirates unjustly wrested from the rightful proprietors must instantly devolve to him. If this be suffered, then, if some pirates should seize a part of Attica, or of Lemnos, or of Imbros, or of Scyros, and if any power should cut them off—the places which they had seized, though our undoubted property, must continue in his possession whose arms chastised these pirates.

Philip is himself sensible of the weakness of this plea. There are others equally sensible of this; but it is imagined easy to impose on you by means of those who are administering our affairs agreeably to the wishes of the Macedonian; who promised him, and are now performing this service. Yet he cannot but know that we must come into possession of this island, in whatever terms our transaction may be expressed, whether you accept it or resume it. Why then should he not use the fair and equitable term, and restore it, rather than adhere to that word which proves his injustice, and pretend to present it as a gift? Not that he may be supposed to confer a benefit on us (such benefits are ridiculous); but that he may demonstrate to all Greece that the Athenians think themselves happy in owing their maritime dominions to the favor of the Macedonian. O, my countrymen, let us not descend to this.

As to his proposal of submitting this contest to umpires, it is the language of derision and mockery. It supposes, in the first place, that we, who are Athenians, could, in our disputes with one sprung from Pella, descend to have our title to the islands determined by arbitration. And if our own power, that power to which Greece owes its liberty, cannot secure us the possession of these places; if umpires are to be appointed; if we are to commit our cause to them; if their votes are absolutely to decide our rights; and if they are to secure to us these islands (provided that they be influenced by Philip's gold)—if such, I say, be your conduct, do you not declare that you have resigned all your power on the continent? Do you not reveal to the world that no attempt can possibly provoke you to oppose him, when for your maritime dominions, whence Athens derives its greatest power, you have not recourse to arms, but submit to umpires?

He further observes, that his commissioners have been sent hither to settle a cartel of commerce; and that this shall be confirmed, not when it has received the sanction of your tribunal, as the law directs, but when it has been returned to him. Thus would he assume a power over your judicature. His intention is to betray you into unguarded concessions, to have it expressly acknowledged in this cartel that you do not accuse him of injuring the State by his outrageous conduct with respect to Potidaea; that you confirm his right both of seizing and possessing this city. And yet those Athenians who had settled in Potidaea—at a time when they were not at war with Philip; when they were united with him in alliance; when the most solemn engagements subsisted between them; when they had the utmost reliance on Philip's oaths—were yet despoiled by this prince of all their possessions. And now he would have you ratify this his iniquitous procedure, and declare that you have suffered no injury, that you have no complaints to urge against him: for that the Macedonians have no need of any cartels in their commerce with the Athenians, former times afford sufficient proof.

Neither Amyntas, the father of Philip, nor any of the other kings of Macedon ever made these cartels with our State, although our intercourse was much greater in those days than now: for Macedon was then subject to us; it paid us tribute; and then, much more than now, did we frequent their markets, and they enjoy the advantages of ours; nor were the tribunals, to which affairs of commerce might be brought, settled in so regular a manner as at present. As these are opened once in each month, they make all cartels between two countries so far removed from each other quite unnecessary. And as these were not agreeable to ancient usage, it is by no means prudent to establish them now, and thus to subject men to the inconvenience of a voyage from Macedon to Athens, or from us to Macedon, in order to obtain justice. The laws of each country are open; and they are sufficient for the decision of all controversies. Be assured, therefore, that by this cartel he means but to betray you into a resignation of all your pretensions to Potidaea.

As to the pirates, he observes that justice requires that we should act in concert with him, in order to guard against those who infest the seas. By this he in effect desires that we should resign to him the sovereignty of the seas, and acknowledge that without Philip's aid we are not able to secure a navigation free and unmolested. Nor is this his only scheme. He would have an uncontrolled liberty of sailing round and visiting the several islands, under the pretence of defending them from pirates, that so he may corrupt the inhabitants, and seduce them from their allegiance to us. Not contented with transporting his exiles to Thasus under the conduct of our commanders, he would gain possession of the other islands by sending out his fleets to sail in company with our admirals, as if united with us in defense of the seas. There are some who say that he has no occasion for a maritime power; yet he who has no occasion to secure such a power prepares his ships for war, erects his arsenals, concerts his naval expeditions, and, by the vast expense bestowed on his marine, plainly shows that it is the grand object of his attention. And can you think, you men of Athens, that Philip could desire you to yield to him this sovereignty of the seas unless he held you in contempt? Unless he had firm reliance on the men whose services he determined to purchase? the men who, insensible to shame, live for Philip, not for their country; who vainly fancy they have enriched their families by the bribes received from him? When these bribes are really the prices for which they have sold their families.

And now with respect to the explanation of the articles of peace, which the ambassadors commissioned by him submitted to our determination (as we insisted only on a point universally acknowledged to be just, that each party should enjoy their own dominions), he denies that ever his ambassadors were commissioned to make, or ever did make, such a concession; so that his partisans must have persuaded him that you have utterly forgotten the declarations made publicly in the assembly. But these of all things cannot possibly be forgotten; for in the very same assembly his ambassadors rose, and made these declarations; and, in consequence of them, the decree was instantly drawn up. As, then, the recital of the decree immediately succeeded the speeches of the ambassadors, it is not possible that you could have recited their declarations falsely. This, then, is an insinuation, not against me, but against the assembly; as if you had transmitted a decree containing an answer to points never once mentioned. But these ambassadors, whose declarations were thus falsified, at the time when we returned our answer in form and invited them to a public entertainment, never once rose up, never once ventured to say, "Men of Athens, we have been misrepresented; you have made us say what we never said"; but acquiesced, and departed.

Recollect, I entreat you, the declarations of Python, who was at the head of this embassy, the man who then received the public thanks of the assembly. They cannot, I presume, have escaped your memory; and they were exactly consonant to Philip's present letter. He accused us of calumniating Philip; he declared that you yourselves were to be blamed; for when his master was endeavoring to do you service, when he preferred your alliance to that of any other of the Grecian States, you defeated his kind intentions by listening to sycophants who wished to receive his money, and yet loaded him with invectives; that when those speeches were repeated to him in which his reputation was so severely treated, and which you heard with such satisfaction, he naturally changed his determination, as he found that he was regarded as devoid of faith by those whom he had resolved to oblige. He desired that the men who spoke in this assembly should not declaim against the peace, which certainly was not to be broken; but that if any article was amiss it should be amended, in which we might be assured of Philip's entire concurrence. But that, if they continued their invectives, without proposing anything by which the treaty might be confirmed and all suspicions of his master removed, then no attention should be given to such men.

You heard these declarations of Python; you assented; you said that they were just; and just they certainly were. But by these professions it was by no means intended to give up an article of the treaty so essential to his interest; to give up what all his treasures had been expended to obtain: no; he had been taught by his instructors of this place that not a man would dare to propose anything contradictory to that decree of Philocrates by which we lost Amphipolis. I, on my part, Athenians, never have presumed to propose anything illegal.

I have, indeed, ventured to speak against the decree of Philocrates, because it was illegal. For this decree, by which Amphipolis was lost, contradicted former decrees, by which our right to this territory was asserted. This, then, was an illegal decree which Philocrates proposed; and, therefore, he who had the due regard to our laws in all that he proposed could not but contradict a decree so inconsistent with our laws. By conforming to the ancient legal acts of this assembly, I showed the due attention to the laws, and at the same time proved that Philip was deceiving you; that he had no intention of amending any article of the treaty; that his sole purpose was to destroy the credit of those speakers who asserted the rights of their country.

It is then manifest, that having first consented to this amendment of the treaty, he now recalls his concession. He insists that Amphipolis is his; that you have acknowledged it to be his by the very words of your decree, which declare that he shall enjoy his own possessions. Such was, indeed, your declaration: but not that Amphipolis was Philip's; for a man may possess the property of others; nor can possession infer a right, since it is frequently acquired by unjust usurpation. So that his argument is no more than an idle sophistical equivocation. He insists particularly on the decree of Philocrates, but he forgets his letter to this State at the time when he laid siege to Amphipolis, in which he directly acknowledged that Amphipolis belonged to you, and declared that his intention in attacking this city was to wrest it from the then possessors, who had no claim to it, and to vest it in the Athenians, who were the rightful sovereigns.

Well, then, the men who were in possession of this city before Philip's conquest usurped our right; but when Philip had reduced it, did our right cease at once? Did he but recover his own dominions? When he reduced Olynthus also, when he subdued Apollonia, when he gained Pallene, did he but recover his own dominions? When he makes use of such evasion, can you think that he is at all solicitous to preserve a decent semblance of reason and justice? No; he treats you with contempt in presuming to dispute your title to a city which the whole nation of Greece, which the Persian king himself by the most authentic declarations acknowledged to be ours.

Another amendment of the treaty which we contended for was this: that all the Greeks not included in the peace should enjoy their liberty and their laws; and that, if invaded, they should be defended by all the confederating parties. For this, I say, we contended, sensible that justice and humanity required not only that we and our allies, and Philip and his allies, should enjoy the advantages of the peace, but that those who were neither allies to Athens nor to Macedon should by no means lie exposed to the oppression of any powerful invader; that they also should derive security from the peace, and that we should in reality lay down our arms and live in general friendship and tranquility. This amendment his letter confesses to be just; you hear that he accepts it. And yet has he overturned the State of the Pheraeans; he has introduced his garrison into the citadel; certainly, that they may enjoy their own laws. His arms are directed against Ambracia. Three cities in Cassopia, Pandosia, Bucheta, and Elatia, all Elean colonies, has he invaded with fire and sword, and reduced to the vassalage of his kinsman Alexander; glorious proofs of his concern for the liberty and independence of the Greeks!

As to those promises of great and important services which he was perpetually lavishing on the State, he now asserts that I have belied and abused him to the Greeks, for that he never once made such promises; so devoid of shame is he, who declared in his letter, which still remains on record, that he would effectually silence his revilers when an accommodation was once obtained, by the number of good offices he would confer on us, and which should be particularly specified whenever he was assured of such an accommodation! These his favors, then, were all provided, and ready to be granted to us when the peace should be concluded; but, when this peace was once concluded, all his favors vanished. How great havoc has been made in Greece you need not be informed. His letters assure us of his gracious intentions to bestow large benefits on us; and now, see the effect of his promises. He refuses to restore our dominions; he claims them as his own. And as to granting us any new dominions, they must not be in this country. No; the Greeks might else be offended. Some other country must be sought for, some foreign land must furnish such grants.

As to those places which he seized in time of peace, in open violation of his engagements, as he has no pretence to urge, as he stands convicted manifestly of injustice, he says that he is ready to submit these points to the decision of an equal and common tribunal. But they are points which, of all others, need no decision. A fair computation of time determines the cause at once. We all know in what month and on what day the peace was made. We all know, too, in what month and on what day Serrium, Ergiske, and the Sacred Mount were taken. The nature and manner of these transactions are no secret. Nor is there need of a tribunal in a point so evident as this, that the peace was made one month before these places were seized.

He asserts that he has returned all your prisoners that were taken. Yet there was one prisoner, a man of Carystus, bound to this city by all the strictest ties, for whose liberty we sent no less than three deputations. Such was Philip's desire to oblige us, that he put this man to death, nay, refused to restore his body for interment.

It is also worthy of attention to consider what was the language of his letters with respect to the Chersonesus, and to compare it with his present actions. All that district which lies beyond the forum he claims as his own, in defiance of our pretensions, and has given the possession to Apollonides the Cardian; and yet the Chersonesus is bounded, not by the forum, but by the altar of Jupiter of the Mountain, which lies in midway between the elm and the chalky shore, where the line was traced for cutting through the Chersonesus. This is evident from the inscription on the altar of Jupiter of the Mountain, which is in these terms:

> Here Jove's fair altar, rais'd by pious hands,
>   Adorns at once and marks the neighboring lands;
> On this side, lo! yon chalky cliffs display'd;
>   On that, the elm extends its awful shade;
> While, in midway, even Heaven's great monarch deigns
>   To point the bound'ries and divide the plains.

This district, then, whose extent is known to many in this assembly, he claims as his property; part of it he himself enjoys, the rest he gives to his creatures; and thus he deprives us of our most valuable possessions. But he is not content with wresting from us all the lands which lie beyond the forum; his letter directs us to come to a judicial decision of any controversy we may have with the Cardians who lie on this side of the forum—with the Cardians, I say, who have presumed to settle in our lands. We have indeed a controversy with these men, and judge you whether the subject be inconsiderable. The lands where they have settled they claim as their just property, and deny our title. The lands that we enjoy they declare are unlawfully usurped; that they themselves are the rightful proprietors; and that their right was acknowledged by a decree proposed by your own citizen Calippus, of the Paenean tribe. He did indeed propose such a decree, for which he was by me impeached of an illegal proceeding; but you suffered him to escape, and thus was your title to these lands rendered disputable and precarious. But if you can submit to a judicial decision of your disputes with the Cardians, what should prevent the other inhabitants of the Chersonesus from demanding the like trial?

With such insolence does he treat you, that he presumes to say, that if the Cardians refuse to be determined by a judicial process, he will compel them; as if we were not able to compel even the Cardians to do us justice. An extraordinary instance this of his regard to Athens!

Yet there are men among you who declare that this letter is very reasonable—men much more deserving of your abhorrence than Philip. His opposition to this State is actuated by the love of glory and power; but citizens of Athens who devote themselves, not to their country, but to Philip, should feel that vengeance which it must be your part to inflict with all severity, unless your brains have forsaken your heads and descended to your heels. It remains that I propose such an answer to this so reasonable letter, and to the declarations of the ambassadors, as may be just and advantageous to the State.

SOURCE: *All the Orations of Demosthenes: Pronounced to Excite the Athenians Against Philip, King of Macedon.* Translated by Thomas Leland. London: W. Johnston. 1757.

DEMOSTHENES

ON THE STATE OF THE CHERSONESUS (342 B.C.)

Demosthenes (see his "The First Philippic" above) continues to try to counter Philip of Macedonia's dominance in Greece. He announces: "I shall speak with an undaunted freedom, for in no other manner can I speak." In spite of Demosthenes, Macedonia conquered the Athenian and Theban armies at the Chersonese peninsula in Thrace (later known as Gallipoli) in 338 B.C.

───────◆───────

It were to be wished, Athenians, that they who speak in public would never suffer hatred or affection to influence their counsels; but, in all that they propose, be directed by unbiased reason; particularly when affairs of state, and those of highest moment, are the object of our attention. But since there are persons whose speeches are partly dictated by a spirit of contention, partly by other like motives, it is your duty, Athenians, to exert that power which your numbers give you, and in all your resolutions and in all your actions to consider only the interest of your country.

Our present concernment is about the affairs of the Chersonesus, and Philip's expedition into Thrace, which has now engaged him eleven months; but most of our orators insist on the actions and designs of Diopithes. As to crimes objected to those men whom our laws can punish when we please, I, for my part, think it quite indifferent whether they be considered now or at some other time; nor is this a point to be violently contested by me or any other speaker. But when Philip, the enemy of our country, is now actually hovering about the Hellespont with a numerous army, and making attempts on our dominions, which, if one moment neglected, the loss may be irreparable; here our attention is instantly demanded; we should resolve, we should prepare with all possible expedition, and not run from our main concern in the midst of foreign clamors and accusations.

I have frequently been surprised at assertions made in public; but never more than when I lately heard it affirmed in the senate, that there are but two expedients to be proposed—either absolutely to declare war, or to continue in peace. The point is this: if Philip acts as one in amity with us; if he does not keep possession of our dominions contrary to his treaty; if he be not everywhere spiriting up enemies against us, all debates are at an end; we are undoubtedly obliged to live in peace, and I find it perfectly agreeable to you. But if the articles of our treaty, ratified by the most solemn oaths, remain on record, open to public inspection; if it appears that long before the departure of Diopithes and his colony, who are now accused of involving us in a war, Philip had unjustly seized many of our possessions (for which I appeal to your own decrees); if, ever since that time, he has been constantly arming himself with all the powers of Greeks and Barbarians to destroy us—what do these men mean who affirm we are either absolutely to declare war, or to observe the peace? You have no choice at all; you have but one just and necessary measure to pursue, which they industriously pass over. And what is this? To repel force by force. Unless they will affirm, that while Philip keeps from Attica and the Piraeus, he does our state no injury, makes no war against us. If it be thus they state the bounds of peace and justice, we must all acknowledge that their sentiments are inconsistent with the common rights of mankind—with the dignity and the safety of Athens.

Besides, they themselves contradict their own accusation of Diopithes. For shall Philip be left at full liberty to pursue all his other designs, provided he keeps from Attica; and shall not Diopithes be permitted to assist the Thracians? And if he does, shall we accuse him of involving us in a war? But this is their incessant cry: "Our foreign troops commit outrageous devastations on the Hellespont: Diopithes, without regard to justice, seizes and plunders vessels! These things must not be suffered." Be it so; I acquiesce! but while they are laboring to have our troops disbanded, by inveighing against that man whose care and industry support them (if they really speak from a regard to justice), they should show us, that if we yield to their remonstrances Philip's army also will be disbanded: but it is apparent that their whole aim is to reduce the state to those circumstances which have occasioned all the losses we have lately suffered. For, be assured of this, that nothing has given Philip such advantage over us as his superior vigilance in improving all opportunities. For, as he is constantly surrounded by his troops, and his mind perpetually engaged in projecting his designs, he can in a moment strike the blow where he pleases. But we wait till some event alarms us; then we are in motion; then we prepare. To this alone I can impute it, that the conquests he has lately made he now enjoys in full security; while all your efforts are too late, all your vast expenses ineffectual; your attempts have served only to discover your enmity and inclination to oppose him; and the consequences of your misconduct are still further aggravated by the disgrace.

Know, then, Athenians, that all our orators allege at present are but words, but idle pretenses. Their whole designs, their whole endeavors are to confine you within the city; that while we have no forces in the field, Philip may be at full liberty to act as he pleases. Consider the present posture of affairs. Philip is now stationed in Thrace, at the head of a large army, and (as we are here informed) sends for reinforcements from Macedon and Thessaly. Now, should he watch the blowing of the Etesian winds, march his forces to Byzantium, and invest it; in the first place, can you imagine that the Byzantines would persist in their present folly; or that they would not have recourse to you for assistance? I cannot think it. No: if there were people in whom they less confided than in us, they would receive even these into their city rather than give it up to him, unless prevented by the quickness of his attack. And should we be unable to sail thither, should there be no forces ready to support them, nothing can prevent their ruin. "But the extravagance and folly of these men exceed all bounds." I grant it. Yet still they should be secured from danger; for this is the interest of our state. Besides, it is by no means clear that he will not march into the Chersonesus itself. On the contrary, if we may judge from the letter which he sent to you, he is determined to oppose us in that country. If then the forces stationed there be still kept up, we may defend our own dominions, and infest those of our enemy; if they be once dispersed and broken, what shall we do if he attempt the

Chersonesus? "Bring Diopithes to a trial." And how will that serve us? "No: but we will dispatch help from here." What if the winds prevent us? "But he will not turn his arms thither." Who will be our surety for this?

Consider, Athenians, is not the season of the year approaching in which it is thought by some that you are to withdraw your forces from the Hellespont, and abandon it to Philip? But suppose (for this too merits our attention) that at his return from Thrace he should neither bend his force against the Chersonesus nor Byzantium, but fall on Chalcis or Megara, as he lately did on Oreum; which would be the wiser course, to oppose him here, and make Attica the seat of war, or to find him employment abroad? I think the latter.

Let these things sink deep into our minds; and let us not raise invidious clamors against those forces which Diopithes is endeavoring to keep up for the service of his country, or attempt to break them: let us rather prepare to reinforce them; grant their general the necessary supplies of money, and in every other instance favor his designs with a hearty zeal. Imagine this question proposed to Philip: "Which would be most agreeable to you, that the forces commanded by Diopithes"—of whatever kind they be, for I shall not dispute on that head—"should continue in full strength and good esteem at Athens, and be reinforced by detachments from the city; or that the clamors and invectives of certain persons should prevail to have them broken and disbanded?" I think he would choose this latter. And are there men among us laboring for that which Philip would entreat the gods to grant him? And if so, is it still a question whence our distresses have arisen?

Let me entreat you to examine the present state of Athens with an unbiased freedom; to consider how we are acting, and how our affairs are conducted. We are neither willing to raise contributions, nor do we dare to take the field, nor do we spare the public funds, nor do we grant supplies to Diopithes, nor do we approve of those subsidies he has procured himself; but we malign him, we pry into his designs, and watch his motions. Thus we proceed, quite regardless of our interests; and while in words we extol those speakers who assert the dignity of their country, our actions favor their opposers. It is usual, when a speaker rises to ask him, "What are we to do?" Give me leave to propose the like question to you: "What am I to say?" For, if you neither raise contributions, nor take the field, nor spare the public funds, nor grant subsidies to Diopithes, nor approve of those provisions he has made himself, nor take the due care of our interests, I have nothing to say. If you grant such unbounded license to informers as even to listen to their accusations of a man for what they pretend he will do, before it be yet done, what can one say?

But it is necessary to explain to some of you the effect of this behavior. (I shall speak with an undaunted freedom, for in no other manner can I speak.) It has been the constant custom of all the commanders who have sailed from this city (if I advance a falsehood let me feel the severest punishment) to take money from the Chians, and from the Erythrians, and from any people that would give it; I mean of the inhabitants of Asia. They who have but one or two ships take a talent; they who command a greater force raise a larger contribution; and the people who give this money, whether more or less, do not give it for nothing (they are not so mad); no, it is the price they pay to secure their trading vessels from rapine and piracy, to provide them with the necessary convoys, and the like, however, they may pretend friendship and affection, and dignify those payments with the name of free gifts.

It is therefore evident, that as Diopithes is at the head of a considerable power, the same contributions will be granted to him. Else how shall he pay his soldiers? How shall he maintain them, who receives nothing from you, and has nothing of his own? From the skies? No; but from what he can collect, and beg, and borrow. So that the whole scheme of his accusers is to warn all people to grant him nothing, as he is to suffer punishment for crimes yet to be committed, not for any he has already committed, or in which he has already assisted. This is the meaning of their clamors. "He is going to form sieges! He leaves the Greeks exposed." Have these men all this tenderness for the Grecian colonies of Asia? They then prefer the interests of foreigners to that of their own country. This must be the case, if they prevail to have another general sent to the Hellespont.

If Diopithes commits outrages—if he be guilty of piracy, one single edict, Athenians—a single edict will put a stop to such proceedings. This is the voice of our laws; that such offenders should be impeached, and not opposed with such vast preparations of ships and money (this would be the height of madness): it is against our enemies, whom the laws cannot touch, that we ought, we must maintain our forces, send out our navies, and raise our contributions. But when citizens have offended, we can decree, we can impeach, we can recall. These are arms sufficient; these are the measures befitting men of prudence: they who would raise disorder and confusion in the state may have recourse to such as these men propose.

But dreadful as it is to have such men among us, yet the most dreadful circumstance of all is this. You assemble here, with minds so disposed, that if anyone accuses Diopithes, or Chares, or Aristophon, or any citizen whatever, as the cause of our misfortunes, you instantly break forth into acclamations and applause. But if a man stands forth, and thus declares the truth: "This is all trifling, Athenians! It is to Philip we owe our calamities: he has plunged us in these difficulties; for had he observed his treaty, our state would be in perfect tranquility!" This you cannot deny; but you hear it with the utmost grief, as if it were the account of some dreadful misfortune. The cause is this (for when I am to urge the interest of my country, let me speak boldly): certain persons who have been intrusted with public affairs have for a long time past rendered you daring and terrible in council, but in all affairs of war wretched and contemptible. Hence it is, that if a citizen, subject to your own power and jurisdiction, be pointed out as the author of your misfortunes, you hear the accusation with applause; but if they are charged on a man who must first be conquered before he can be punished, then you are utterly disconcerted; that truth is too severe to be borne. Your ministers, Athenians, should take a quite contrary course. They should render you gentle and humane in council, where the rights of citizens and allies come before you; in military affairs they should inspire you with fierceness and intrepidity; for here you are engaged with enemies, with armed troops. But now, by leading you gently on to their purposes, by the most abject compliance with your humors, they have so formed and molded you that in your assemblies you are delicate, and attend but to flattery and entertainment, in your affairs you find yourselves threatened with extremity of danger.

And now, in the name of Heaven, suppose that the states of Greece should thus demand an account of those opportunities which your indolence has lost: "Men of Athens! You are ever sending embassies to us; you assure us that Philip is projecting our ruin, and that, of all the Greeks, you warn us to guard against this man's designs." (And it is too true we have done thus.) "But, O most wretched of mankind, when this man has been ten months detained abroad; when sickness, and the severity of winter, and the armies of his enemies rendered it impossible for him to return home, you neither restored the liberty of Euboea nor recovered any of your own dominions. But while you sit at home in perfect ease and health (if such a state may be called health), Euboea is commanded by his two tyrants; the one, just opposite to Attica, to keep you perpetually in awe; the other to Scyathus. Yet you have not attempted to oppose even this. No; you have submitted; you have been insensible to your wrongs; you have fully declared that if Philip were ten times to die, it would not inspire you with the least degree of vigor. Why, then, these embassies, these accusations, all this unnecessary trouble to us?" If they should say this, what could we allege? What answer could we give? I know not.

We have those among us who think a speaker fully confuted by asking, "What, then, is to be done?" To whom I answer, with the utmost truth and justness, "Not what we are now doing." But I shall be more explicit if they will be as ready to follow as to ask advice.

First then, Athenians, be firmly convinced of these truths: that Philip does commit hostilities against us, and has violated the peace (and let us no longer accuse each other of his crimes); that he is the implacable enemy of this whole city, of the ground on which this city stands, of every inhabitant within these walls, even of those who imagine themselves highest in his favor. If they doubt this, let them think of Euthycrates and Lasthenes, the Olynthians. They who seemed the nearest to his heart, the moment they betrayed their country were distinguished only by the superior cruelty of their death. But it is against our constitution that his arms are principally directed; nor, in all his schemes, in all his actions, has he anything so immediately in view as to subvert it. And there is some sort of a necessity for this. He knows full well that his conquests, however great and extensive, can never be secure while you continue free; but that, if once he meets with any accident (and every man is subject to many), all those whom he has forced into his service will instantly revolt, and fly to you for protection; for you are not naturally disposed to grasp at empire yourselves, but to frustrate the ambitious attempts of others; to be ever ready to oppose usurpation, and assert the liberty of mankind; this is your peculiar character. And therefore it is not without regret that he sees in your freedom a spy on the incidents of his fortune. Nor is this his reasoning weak or trivial.

In the first place, therefore, we are to consider him as the enemy of our state, the implacable enemy of our free constitution. Nothing but the deepest sense of this can give you a true, vigorous, and active spirit. In the next place, be assured that everything he is now laboring upon, everything he is concerting, he is concerting against our city; and that wherever any man opposes him, he opposes an attempt against these walls; for none of you can be weak enough to imagine that Philip's desires are centered in those paltry villages of Thrace (for what name else can one give to Drongilus, and Cabyle, and Mastira, and all those places he is now reducing to his obedience?); that he endures the severity of toils and seasons, and braves the utmost dangers for these, and has no designs on the ports, and the arsenals, and the navies, and the silver mines, and all the other revenues of Athens, but that he will leave them for you to enjoy; while for some wretched hoards of grain in the cells of Thrace he takes up his winter quarters in the horrors of a dungeon. Impossible! No; these and all his expeditions are really intended to facilitate the conquest of Athens.

Let us, then, approve ourselves men of wisdom; and, fully persuaded of these truths, let us shake off our extravagant and dangerous supineness; let us supply the necessary expenses; let us call on our allies; let us take all possible measures for keeping up a regular army; so that, as he has his force constantly prepared to injure and enslave the Greeks, yours too may be ever ready to protect and assist them. If you depend on occasional detachments you cannot ever expect the least degree of success; you must keep an army constantly on foot, provide for its maintenance, appoint public treasurers, and by all possible means secure your military funds; and while these officers account for all disbursements, let your generals be bound to answer for the conduct of the war. Let these be your measures, these your resolutions, and you will compel Philip to live in the real observance of an equitable peace, and to confine himself to his own kingdom (which is most for our interest), or we shall fight him on equal terms.

If any man thinks that the measures I propose will require great expense, and be attended with much toil and trouble, he thinks justly. Yet let him consider what consequences must attend the state if these measures be neglected, and it will appear that we shall really be gainers by engaging heartily in this cause. Suppose some god should be our surety (for no mortal ought to be relied on in an affair of such moment) that, if we continue quiet, and give up all our interests, he will not at last turn his arms against us; it would yet be shameful; it would (I call all the powers of Heaven to witness!) be unworthy of you, unworthy of the dignity of your country, and the glory of your ancestors, to abandon the rest of Greece to slavery for the sake of private ease. I, for my part, would die rather than propose so mean a conduct: however, if there be any other person who will recommend it, be it so; neglect your defense; give up your interests! But if there be no such counselor; if, on the contrary, we all foresee that the farther this man is suffered to extend his conquests, the more formidable and powerful enemy we must find in him, why this reluctance? Why do we delay? Or when, my countrymen, will we perform our duty? Must some necessity compel us? What one may call the necessity of freemen not only presses us now, but has long since been felt: that of slaves, it is to be wished, may never approach us. And how do these differ? To a freeman, the disgrace of past misconduct is the most urgent necessity; to a slave stripes and bodily pains. Far be this from us! It ought not to be mentioned.

I would now gladly lay before you the whole conduct of certain politicians; but I spare them. One thing only I shall observe: the moment that Philip is mentioned there is still one ready to start up, and cry, "What a happiness to live in peace! How grievous the maintenance of a great army! Certain persons have designs on our treasury!" Thus they delay their resolutions, and give him full liberty to act as he pleases; hence you gain ease and indulgence for the present (which I fear may at some time prove too dear a purchase); and these men recommend themselves to your favor, and are well paid for their service.

But in my opinion there is no need to persuade you to peace, who sit down already thoroughly persuaded. Let it be recommended to him who is committing hostilities; if he can be prevailed on, you are ready to concur. Nor should we think those expenses grievous which our security requires, but the consequences which must arise if such expenses be denied. Then as to plundering our treasury; this must be prevented by intrusting it to proper guardians, not by neglecting our affairs. For my own part, Athenians, I am filled with indignation when I find some persons expressing their impatience, as if our treasures were exposed to plunderers, and yet utterly unaffected at the progress of Philip, who is successively plundering every state of Greece; and this, that he may at last fall with all his fury on you.

What, then, can be the reason, Athenians, that, notwithstanding all his manifest hostilities, all his acts of violence, all the places he has taken from us, these men will not acknowledge that he has acted unjustly, and that he is at war with us, but accuse those of embroiling you in a war who call on you to oppose him and to check his progress? I shall tell you. That popular resentment which may arise from any disagreeable circumstances with which a war may be attended (and it is necessary, absolutely necessary that a war should be attended with many such disagreeable circumstances) they would cast on your faithful counselors, that you may pass sentence on them, instead of opposing Philip; and they turn accusers instead of meeting the punishment due to their present practices. This is the meaning of their clamors that certain persons would involve you in a war: hence have they raised all these cavils and debates.

I know full well that before any Athenian had ever moved you to declare war against him, Philip had seized many of our dominions, and has now sent assistance to the Cardians. If you are resolved to dissemble your sense of his hostilities, he would be the weakest of mankind if he attempted to contradict you. But suppose he marches directly against us, what shall we say in that case? He will still assure us that he is not at war; such were his professions to the people of Oreum when his forces were in the heart of their country; and to those of Pherae, until the moment that he attacked their walls; and thus he at first amused the Olynthians, until he had marched his army into their territory. And will you still insist, even in such a case, that they who call on us to defend our country are embroiling us in a war? Then slavery is inevitable. There is no other medium between an obstinate refusal to take arms on your part, and a determined resolution to attack us on the part of our enemy.

Nor is the danger which threatens us the same with that of other people. It is not the conquest of Athens which Philip aims at: no, it is our utter extirpation. He knows full well that slavery is a state you would not, or, if you were inclined, you could not submit to; for sovereignty is become habitual to you. Nor is he ignorant that, at any unfavorable juncture, you have more power to obstruct his enterprises than the whole world besides.

Let us then be assured that we are contending for the very being of our state; let this inspire us with abhorrence of those who have sold themselves to this man, and let them feel the severity of public justice; for it is not possible to conquer our foreign enemy until we have punished those traitors who are serving him within our walls. Else, while we strike on these as so many obstacles, our enemies must necessarily prove superior to us. And whence is it that he dares treat you with insolence (I cannot give his present conduct any other name); that he utters menaces against you, while on others he confers acts of kindness (to deceive them at least, if for no other purpose)? Thus, by heaping favors on the Thessalians, he has reduced them to their present slavery. It is not possible to recount the various artifices by which he abused the wretched Olynthians, from his first insidious gift of Potidaea. But now he seduced the Thebans to his party, by making them masters of Boeotia, and easing them of a great and grievous war. And thus, by being gratified in some favorite point, these people are either involved in calamities known to the whole world, or wait with submission for the moment when such calamities are to fall on them.

I do not recount all that you yourselves have lost, Athenians; but in the very conclusion of the peace, how have you been deceived? how have you been despoiled? Was not Phocis, was not Thermopylae, were not our Thracian dominions, Doriscum, Serrium, and even our ally Cersobleptes, all wrested from us? Is he not at this time in possession of Cardia? And does he not avow it? Whence is it, I say, that he treats you in so singular a manner? Because ours is the only state where there is allowed full liberty to plead the cause of enemy; and the man who sells his country may harangue securely, at the very time that you are despoiled of your dominions. It was not safe to speak for Philip at Olynthus until the people of Olynthus had been gained by the surrender of Potidaea. In Thessaly it was not safe to speak for Philip until the Thessalians had been gained by the expulsion of the tyrants and the recovery of their rank of amphictyons; nor could it have been safely attempted at Thebes before he had restored Boeotia and extirpated the Phocians. But at Athens, although he has robbed us of Amphipolis and the territory of Cardia; though he awes us with his fortifications in Euboea; though he be now on his march to Byzantium; yet his partisans may speak for Philip without any danger. Hence, some of them, from the meanest poverty, have on a sudden risen to affluence; some, from obscurity and disgrace, to eminence and honor; while you, on the contrary, from glory, have sunk into meanness; from riches, to poverty; for the riches of a state I take to be its allies, its credit, its connections, in all which you are poor. And by your neglect of these, by your utter insensibility to your wrongs, he is become fortunate and great, the terror of Greeks and Barbarians; and you abandoned and despised; splendid indeed in the abundance of your markets; but as to any real provision for your security, ridiculously deficient.

There are some orators, I find, who view your interests and their own in a quite different light. They would persuade you to continue quiet, whatever injuries are offered to you, they themselves cannot be quiet, though no one offers them the least injury. When one of these men rises, I am sure to hear, "What! Will you not propose your decree? Will you not venture? No; you are timid: you want true spirit." I own, indeed, I am not, nor would I choose to be, a bold, an importune, an audacious speaker. And yet, if I mistake not, I have more real courage than they who manage your affairs with this rash hardiness. For he who, neglecting the public interests, is engaged only in trials, in confiscations, in rewarding, in accusing, does not act from any principle of courage, but as he never speaks but to gain your favor, never proposes measures that are attended with the least hazard; in this he has a pledge of his security, and therefore is he daring. But he who for his country's good often opposes your inclinations; who gives the most salutary, though not always the most agreeable counsel; who pursues those measures whose success depends more on fortune than on prudence, and is yet willing to be accountable for the event; this is the man of courage; this is the true patriot: not they who, by flattering your passions, have lost the most important interests of the state—men whom I am so far from imitating, or deeming citizens of worth, that should this question be proposed to me, "What services have you done your country?" Though I might recount the galleys I have fitted out, and the public entertainments I have exhibited and the contributions I have paid, and the captives I have ransomed, and many like acts of benevolence, I would yet pass them all by, and only say that my public conduct has ever been directly opposite to theirs.

I might, like them, have turned accuser, have distributed rewards and punishments; but this is a part I never assumed; my inclinations were averse; nor could wealth or honors prompt me to it. No; I confine myself to such counsels as have sunk my reputation; but, if pursued, must raise the reputation of my country. Thus much I may be allowed to say without exposing myself to envy. I should not have thought myself a good citizen had I proposed such measures as would have made me the first among my countrymen, but reduced you to the last of states; on the contrary, the faithful minister should raise the glory of his country, and on all occasions advise the most salutary, not the easiest measures. To these nature itself inclines; those are not to be promoted but by the utmost efforts of a wise and faithful counselor.

I have heard it objected, "That indeed I ever speak with reason; yet still this is no more than words—that the state requires something more effectual, some vigorous actions." On which I shall give my sentiments without the least reserve. The sole business of a speaker is, in my opinion, to propose the course you are to pursue. This were easy to be proved. You know that when the great Timotheus moved you to defend the Euboeans against the tyranny of Thebes, he addressed you thus: "What, my countrymen! When the Thebans are actually in the island, are you deliberating what is to be done? What part to be taken? Will you not cover the seas with your navies? Why are you not at the Piraeus? Why are you not embarked?" Thus Timotheus advised; thus you acted, and success ensued. But had he spoken with the same spirit, and had your indolence prevailed, and his advice been rejected, would the state have had the same success? By no means. And so in the present case: vigor and execution is your part; from your speakers you are only to expect wisdom and integrity.

I shall just give the summary of my opinion, and then descend. You should raise supplies; you should keep up your present forces, and reform whatever abuses may be found in them (not break them entirely on the first complaint). You should send ambassadors into all parts, to reform, to remonstrate, to exert all their efforts in the service of the state. But, above all things, let those corrupt ministers feel the severest punishment; let them, at all times, and in all places, be the objects of your abhorrence: that wise and faithful counselors may appear to have consulted their own interests as well as that of others. If you will act thus, if you will shake off this indolence, perhaps, even yet, perhaps, we may promise ourselves some good fortune. But if you only just exert yourselves in acclamations and applauses, and when anything is to be done sink again into your supineness, I do not see how all the wisdom of the world can save the state from ruin when you deny your assistance.

SOURCE: *All the Orations of Demosthenes: Pronounced to Excite the Athenians Against Philip, King of Macedon*. Translated by Thomas Leland. London: W. Johnston. 1757.

LUCIUS LENTULUS

ON TREATING WITH THE SAMNITES
(321 B.C.)

Titus Livius Patavinus (c. 59 B.C.–17 A.D.), known more commonly in English as Livy, recounted centuries of Roman history. Here he tells of an incident in the midst of the Second Samnite War (326–304 B.C.), when two Roman armies invaded Samnite territory and were trapped. They surrendered themselves and two cities to the Samnites, a people on the southern Italian peninsula, and were sent back stripped of their weapons and equipment to Rome. Lucius Lentulus, a Roman lieutenant about whom nothing else is known, defended the surrender. Eighteen hundred years later, the Italian philosopher Niccolo Machiavelli reflected on this very incident in his *Discourses on Livy*.

Consuls, I have often heard my father say that he was the only man in the Capitol who did not advise the senators to ransom the State from the Gauls with gold; and he would not concur in this because they had not been enclosed with a trench and rampart by the enemy (who were remarkably slothful with respect to works and raising fortifications), and because they might sally forth, if not without great danger, yet without certain destruction.

Now if, in like manner as they had it in their power to rush in arms from the Capitol against their foe, as men besieged have often sallied out on the besiegers, so it were possible for us to come to blows with the enemy, either on equal or on unequal ground, I would not be wanting in the high quality of my father's spirit in stating my advice. I acknowledge, indeed, that death in defense of our country is highly glorious; and I am ready either to devote myself for the Roman people and the legions, or to plunge into the midst of the enemy. But in this spot I behold my country; in this spot I behold the whole of the Roman legions: and unless these choose to rush on death in defense of their own individual characters, what is there which can be preserved by their death? The houses of the city, some may say, and the walls of it, and the crowd dwelling in it, by whom the city is inhabited. But in fact, in case of the destruction of this army, all these are betrayed, not preserved. For who will protect them? An unwarlike and unarmed multitude, shall I suppose? Yes, just as they defended them against the attacks of the Gauls. Will they call to their succor an army from Veii, with Camillus at its head?

Here, on the spot, are our hopes and strength; by preserving them we preserve our country; by delivering them to death, we abandon and betray our country. But to surrender is shameful and ignominious. True; but such ought to be our affection for our country that we should save it by our own disgrace, if necessity required, as freely as by our death. Let, therefore, that indignity be undergone, howsoever great, and let us submit to that necessity which even the gods themselves do not overcome. Go, consuls, ransom for arms the State which your ancestors ransomed with gold.

SOURCE: *Orators of Ancient Rome*. Guy Carleton Lee. New York: G. P. Putnam's Sons. 1900.

P. CORNELIUS SCIPIO

TO HIS SOLDIERS (218 B.C.)

In his account of the Second Punic War (218–201 B.C.), Livy narrates the Roman consul Scipio's brave speech preceding a devastating defeat at the hands of Hannibal's Carthaginians. Scipio went on to win important victories for Rome, but was killed in battle in 212 B.C.

―――――◦―――――

If, soldiers, I were leading out to battle that army which I had with me in Gaul, I should have thought it superfluous to address you; for of what use would it be to exhort either those horsemen who so gloriously vanquished the cavalry of the enemy at the river Rhone, or those legions with whom, pursuing this very enemy flying before us, I obtained, in lieu of victory, a confession of superiority, shown by his retreat and refusal to fight? But now because that army, levied for the province of Spain, maintains the war under my auspices and the command of my brother, Cneius Scipio, in the country where the Senate and the people of Rome wished him to serve; and since I have offered myself voluntarily for this contest, that you might have a consul for your leader against Hannibal and the Carthaginians, a few words are required to be addressed from a new commander to soldiers unacquainted with him.

That you may not be ignorant of the nature either of the war or of the enemy, let me remind you, soldiers, that you have to fight with those whom in the former war you conquered both by land and sea; from whom you have exacted tribute for twenty years;

114

from whom you hold Sicily and Sardinia, taken as the prizes of victory. In the present contest, therefore, you and they will have those feelings which are wont to belong to the victors and the vanquished. They are now about to fight, not because they are daring, but because it is unavoidable; unless you can believe that those who declined the engagement when their forces were entire should have now gained more confidence when two-thirds of their infantry and cavalry have been lost in the passage of the Alps, and when almost greater numbers have perished than survive. Yes, they are few, indeed (some may say), but they are vigorous in mind and body; men whose strength and power almost no force may withstand. On the contrary, they are but the semblances, nay, they are rather the shadows of men; for they are worn out with hunger, cold, dirt, and filth, and bruised and enfeebled among stones and rocks. Besides all this, their joints are frost-bitten, their sinews stiffened with the snow, their limbs withered up by the frost, their armor battered and gaping, their horses lame and powerless. With such cavalry, with such infantry, you have to fight; you will not have enemies in reality, but rather their last remains. And I fear nothing more than that when you have fought Hannibal, the Alps may appear to have conquered him. But perhaps it was fitting that the gods themselves should, without any human aid, commence and carry forward a war against a leader and a people who violate the faith of treaties; and that we, who have been injured next to the gods, should finish the contest thus commenced and now nearly completed.

I do not fear lest anyone should think that I say this ostentatiously for the sake of encouraging you, while in my own mind I am differently affected. I was at liberty to go with my army into Spain, my own province, whither I had already set out. There I should have had a brother as a sharer of my councils and my dangers, and Hasdrubal for my antagonist, and without question a less laborious war. Nevertheless, as I sailed along the coast of Gaul, I landed on hearing of this enemy, and having sent forward the cavalry, I moved my camp to the Rhone. In a battle of cavalry, for with that part of my forces the opportunity was afforded of engaging, I routed the enemy; and because I could not overtake by land his army of infantry, which was rapidly hurried away as if in flight, having returned to the ships with all the speed I could, after compassing such an extent of sea and land, I have met him at the foot of the Alps.

Do I appear to have fallen in unexpectedly with this dreaded foe while declining the contest, or to encounter him in his track, to challenge him and drag him out to decide the contest? I am anxious to try whether the earth has suddenly, in these twenty years, sent forth a new race of Carthaginians, or whether these are the same who fought at the islands of Agates, and whom you permitted to depart from Eryx, valued at eighteen denarii a head; and whether this Hannibal be, as he himself gives out, the rival of the expeditions of Hercules, or one left by his father the tributary, the subject and the slave of the Roman people; who, if his guilt at Saguntum did not drive him to frenzy, would certainly reflect, if not upon his conquered country, at least on his family, his father, and the treaties written by the hand of Hamilcar; who, at the command of our consul, withdrew the garrison from Eryx; who, indignant and grieving, submitted to the harsh conditions imposed on the conquered Carthaginians; who agreed to depart from Sicily and pay tribute to the Roman people.

I would therefore have you fight, soldiers, not only with that spirit with which you are wont to encounter other enemies, but with a certain indignation and resentment, as if you saw your slaves suddenly taking up arms against you. We might have killed them, when shut up in Eryx, by hunger, the most dreadful of human tortures; we might have carried our victorious fleet over to Africa, and in a few days have destroyed Carthage without any opposition. We granted pardon to their prayers; we released them from the blockade; we made peace with them when conquered; and we afterwards considered them under our protection when they were oppressed by the African war.

In return for these benefits, they come, under the command of a furious youth, to attack our country. And I wish that the contest on your side was for glory, and not for safety. It is not about the possession of Sicily and Sardinia, concerning which the dispute was formerly, but for Italy, that you must fight; nor is there another army behind, which, if we should not conquer, can resist the enemy; nor are there other Alps, during the passage of which fresh forces may be procured.

Here, soldiers, we must make our stand, as if we fought beneath the walls of Rome. Let everyone consider that he defends with his weapons not only his own person, but his wife and young children; nor let him only entertain domestic cares and anxieties, but at the same time let him bear in mind that the Senate and people of Rome are now anxiously regarding our efforts; and that, according to what our strength and valor shall be, such henceforward will be the fortune of that city and of the Roman Empire.

Source: *Orators of Ancient Rome*. Guy Carleton Lee. New York: G. P. Putnam's Sons. 1900.

MARCUS JUNIUS *Versus*
TITUS MANLIUS TORQUATUS

ON RANSOMING THE PRISONERS
(216 B.C.)

The Roman Republic's Second Punic War (218–201 B.C.), against Hannibal's Carthaginians, went poorly at first. The battle at Cannae was a disaster, with 70,000 Romans killed and 9,000 captured or fled. When Hannibal gave the captives leave to return to Rome to obtain ransom, Marcus Junius, a spokesman for the captives, affectingly—and seemingly persuasively—addressed the Senate. He was answered by Titus Manlius Torquatus.

———◆———

[Marcus Junius]

There is not one of us, Conscript Fathers, who is not aware that there never was a nation which held prisoners in greater contempt than our own. But unless our own cause is dearer to us than it should be, never did men fall into the hands of the enemy who less deserved to be disregarded than we do; for we did not surrender our arms in battle through fear; but having prolonged the battle almost till nightfall, standing upon heaps of our slaughtered countrymen, we betook ourselves to our camp. For the remainder of the day and during the following night, although exhausted with exertions and wounds, we protected our ramparts. On the following day, when beset by the enemy, we were deprived of water, and there was no hope of breaking through the dense bands of the enemy; and moreover, not considering it an impiety that any Roman soldier should survive the battle of Cannae, after fifty thousand of our army had been butchered; then at length we agreed upon terms on which we might be ransomed and let off; and our arms, in which there was no longer any protection, we delivered to the enemy. We had been informed that our ancestors also had redeemed themselves from the Gauls with gold, and that though so rigid as to the terms of peace, had sent ambassadors to Tarentum for the purpose of ransoming the captives. And yet both the fight at the Allia with the Gauls, and at Heraclea with Pyrrhus, was disgraceful, not so much on account of the loss as on account of the panic and flight.

Heaps of Roman corpses cover the plains of Cannae; not would any of us have survived the battle, had not the enemy wanted the strength and the sword to slay us. There are, too, some of us who did not even retreat from the field, but, being left to guard the camp, came into the hands of the enemy when it was surrendered. For my part, I envy not the good fortune or condition of any citizen or fellow-soldier, nor would I endeavor to raise myself by depressing another: but not even those men who, for the most part, leaving their arms, fled from the field, and stopped not till they arrived at Venusia or Canusium; not even those men, unless some reward is due to them on account of their swiftness of foot and running, would justly set themselves before us or boast that there is more protection to the State in them than in us. But you will find them to be both good and brave soldiers, and us still more zealous, because, by your kindness, we shall have been ransomed and restored to our country. You are levying from every age and condition: I hear that eight thousand slaves are being armed. We are no fewer in number; nor will the expense of redeeming us be greater than that of purchasing these. Should I compare ourselves with them, I should injure the name of a Roman.

I should think also, Conscript Fathers, that in deliberating on such a measure, it ought also to be considered (if you are disposed to be over severe, which you cannot do from any demerit of ours) to what sort of enemy you would abandon us. Is it to Pyrrhus, for instance, who treated us, when his prisoners, like guests; or to a barbarian and Carthaginian, of whom it is difficult to determine whether his rapacity or cruelty be the greater? If you were to see the chains, the squalid appearance, the loathsomeness of your

countrymen, that spectacle would not, I am confident, less affect
you than if, on the other hand, you beheld your legions prostrate
on the plains of Cannae. You may behold the solicitude and the
tears of our kinsmen, as they stand in the lobby of your Senate-
house and await your answer. When they are in so much suspense
and anxiety in behalf of us, and those who are absent, what think
you must be our own feelings, whose lives and liberty are at stake?

By Hercules! should Hannibal himself, contrary to his nature, be
disposed to be lenient towards us, yet we should not consider our
lives worth possessing, since we have seemed unworthy of being
ransomed by you. Formerly, prisoners dismissed by Pyrrhus, without ransom, returned to Rome; but they returned in company with
ambassadors, the chief men of the State, who were sent to ransom
them. Would I return to my country, a citizen, and not considered
worth three hundred denarii? Every man has his own way of thinking, Conscript Fathers. I know that my life and person are at stake.
But the danger which threatens my reputation affects me most, if
we should go away rejected and condemned by you; for men will
never suppose that you grudged the price of our redemption.

[Livy's narration:] *When he had finished his address, the crowd of persons in the comitium immediately set up a loud lamentation, and stretched
out their hands to the senate, imploring them to restore to them their children, their brothers, and their kinsmen. Their fears and affection for their
kindred had brought the women also with the crowd of men in the forum.
Witnesses being excluded, the matter began to be discussed in the senate.
There being a difference of opinion, and some advising that they should be
ransomed at the public charge, others, that the state should be put to no
expense, but that they should not be prevented redeeming themselves at
their own cost; and that those who had not the money at present should
receive a loan from the public coffer, and security given to the people by their
sureties and properties; Titus Manlius Torquatus, a man of primitive, and,
as some considered, over-rigorous severity, being asked his opinion, is
reported thus to have spoken:*

[Titus Manlius Torquatus]

Had the deputies confined themselves to making a request, in
behalf of those who are in the hands of the enemy, that they
might be ransomed, I should have briefly given my opinion,

without inveighing against anyone. For what else would have been necessary but to admonish you, that you ought to adhere to the custom handed down from your ancestors, a precedent indispensable to military discipline. But now, since they have almost boasted of having surrendered themselves to the enemy, and have claimed to be preferred, not only to those who were captured by the enemy in the field, but to those also who came to Venusia and Canusium, and even to the consul Terentius himself, I will not suffer you to remain in ignorance of things which were done there. And I could wish that what I am about to bring before you were stated at Canusium, before the army itself, the best witness of every man's cowardice or valor; or at least that one person, Publius Sempronius, were here, whom, had they followed as their leader, they would this day have been soldiers in the Roman camp, and not prisoners in the power of the enemy. But though the enemy was fatigued with fighting, and engaged in rejoicing for their victory, and had, the greater part of them, retired into their camp, and they had the night at their disposal for making a sally, and as they were seven thousand armed troops, might have forced their way through the troops of the enemy, however closely arrayed; yet they neither of themselves attempted to do this, nor were willing to follow another.

Throughout nearly the whole night Sempronius ceased not to admonish and exhort them, while but few of the enemy were about the camp, while there was stillness and quiet, while the night would conceal their design, that they would follow him; that before daybreak they might reach places of security, the cities of their allies. If as Publius Decius, the military tribune in Samnium, said, within the memory of our grandfathers; if he had said, as Calpurnius Flamma, in the first Punic war, when we were youths, said to the three hundred volunteers, when, he was leading them to seize upon an eminence situated in the midst of the enemy: *"Let us die, soldiers, and by our deaths rescue the surrounded legions from ambuscade!"*

If Publius Sempronius had said thus, he would neither have considered you as Romans nor men, had no one stood forward as his companion in so valorous an attempt. He points out to you the road that leads not to glory more than to safety; he restores you to your country, your parents, your wives and children. Do you want courage to effect your preservation? What would you do if you had to die for your country? Fifty thousand of your countrymen and allies on that very day lay around you slain. If so many examples of courage did not move you, nothing ever will. If so great a carnage did not make life less dear, none ever will. While in freedom and safety, show your affection for your country; nay, rather do so while it is your country, and you its citizens. Too late you now endeavor to evince your regard for her when degraded, disfranchised from the rights of citizens, and become the slaves of the Carthaginians. Shall you return by purchase to that degree which you have forfeited by cowardice and neglect?

You did not listen to Sempronius, your countryman, when he bid you take arms and follow him; but a little after you listened to Hannibal, when he ordered your arms to be surrendered, and your camp betrayed. But why do I charge those men with cowardice, when I might tax them with villainy? They not only refused to follow him who gave them good advice, but endeavored to oppose and hold him back, had not some men of the greatest bravery, drawing their swords, removed the cowards. Publius Sempronius, I say, was obliged to force his way through a band of his countrymen, before he burst through the enemy's troops. Can our country regret such citizens as these, whom if all the rest resembled, she would not have one citizen of all those who fought at Cannae? Out of seven thousand armed men, there were six hundred who had courage to force their way, who returned to their country free, and in arms; nor did forty-thousand of the enemy successfully oppose them. How safe, think you, would a passage have been for nearly two legions? Then you would have had this day at Canusium, conscript fathers, twenty thousand bold and faithful.

But now how can these men be called faithful and good citizens (for they do not even call themselves brave), except any man suppose that they showed themselves such when they opposed those who were desirous of forcing their way through the enemy? Or, unless any man can suppose, that they do not envy those men their safety and glory acquired by valor, when they must know that their timidity and cowardice were the cause of their ignominious servitude? Skulking in their tents, they preferred to wait for the light and the enemy together, when they had an opportunity of sallying forth during the silence of the night. But though they had not courage to sally forth from the camp, had they courage to defend it strenuously? Having endured a siege for several days and nights, did they protect their rampart by their arms, and themselves by their rampart? At length, having dared and suffered every extremity, every support of life being gone, their strength exhausted with famine, and unable to hold their arms, were they subdued by the necessities of nature, rather than by arms? At sunrise, the enemy approached the rampart: before the second hour, without hazarding any contest, they delivered up their arms and themselves.

Here is their military service for you during two days. When they ought to have stood firm in array and fight on, then they fled back into their camp; when they ought to have fought before their rampart, they delivered up their camp: good for nothing, either in the field or the camp. I redeem you?

When you ought to sally from the camp, you linger and hesitate; and when you ought to stay and protect your camp in arms, you surrender the camp, your arms, and yourselves to the enemy. I am of opinion, conscript fathers, that these men should no more be ransomed, than that those should be surrendered to Hannibal, who sallied from the camp through the midst of the enemy, and, with the most distinguished courage, restored themselves to their country.

[Livy's narrative:] *After Manlius had thus spoken, notwithstanding the captives were related to many even of the senators, besides the practice of the state, which had never shown favor to captives, even from the remotest times, the sum of money also influenced them: for they were neither willing to drain the treasury, a large sum of money having been already issued for buying and arming slaves to serve in the war, nor to enrich Hannibal, who, according to report, was particularly in want of this very thing. The sad reply, that the captives would not be ransomed, being delivered, and fresh grief being added to the former on account of the loss of so many citizens, the people accompanied the deputies to the gate with copious tears and lamentations.*

SOURCE: *The History of Rome by Titus Livius*. Translated by D. Spillan and Cyrus Edmonds. London: Henry G. Bohn. 1849.

CAIUS MEMMIUS

AGAINST THE POWER OF THE NOBILITY (C. 110 B.C.)

During the Jurgurthine War (112–106 B.C.), Memmius called out aristocrats for corruption: "But who are these, who have thus taken the government into their hands? Men of the most abandoned character, of blood-stained hands, of insatiable avarice, of enormous guilt, and of matchless pride; men by whom integrity, reputation, public spirit, and indeed everything, whether honorable or dishonorable, is converted to a means of gain." As a candidate for consul in 100 B.C., Memmius was killed by a mob. The historian Sallust (Gaius Sallustius Crispus), who presents this speech, was born c. 86 B.C.

[Sallust's narrative:] *When rumor had made known the affairs transacted in Africa [the conduct of the Roman generals in treating with Jugurtha] and the mode in which they had been brought to pass, the conduct of the consul became a subject of discussion in every place and company at Rome. Among the people there was violent indignation; as to the Senators, it was a matter of doubt whether they would ratify so flagitious a proceeding or annul the act of the consul. The influence of Scaurus, who was said to be the supporter and accomplice of Bestia, was what chiefly restrained the Senate from acting with justice and honor. But Caius Memmius, of whose boldness of spirit and hatred to the power of the nobility I have already spoken, incited the people by his harangues, during the perplexity and delay of the Senators, to take vengeance on the authors of the treaty; he exhorted them not to abandon the public interest or their own liberty; he set before them the many tyrannical and violent proceedings of the nobles, and omitted no art to inflame the popular passions. As the eloquence of Memmius, at that period, had great reputation and influence, I have thought proper to give in full one out of many of his speeches; and I take, in preference to others, that which he delivered in the assembly of the people, after the return of Bestia, in words of the following effect:*

Were not my zeal for the good of the state, my fellow-citizens, superior to every other feeling, there are many considerations which would deter me from appearing in your cause; I allude to the power of the opposite party, your own tameness of spirit, the absence of all justice, and, above all, the fact that integrity is attended with more danger than honor. Indeed, it grieves me to relate how, during the last fifteen years, you have been a sport to the arrogance of an oligarchy; how dishonorably and how utterly unavenged your defenders have perished; and how your spirit has become degenerate by sloth and indolence; for not even now, when your enemies are in your power, will you rouse yourselves to action, but continue still to stand in awe of those to whom you should be a terror.

Yet, notwithstanding this state of things, I still feel prompted to make an attack on the power of that faction. That liberty of speech, therefore, which has been left me by my father, I shall assuredly exert against them; but whether I shall use it in vain, or for your advantage, must, my fellow-citizens, depend upon yourselves. I do not, however, exhort you, as your ancestors have often done, to rise in arms against injustice. There is at present no need of violence, no need of secession; for your tyrants must work their fall by their own misconduct.

After the murder of Tiberius Gracchus, whom they accused of aspiring to be king, persecutions were instituted against the common people of Rome; and after the slaughter of Caius Gracchus and Marcus Fulvius, many of your order were put to death in prison. But let us leave these proceedings out of the question; let us admit that to restore their rights to the people was to aspire to sovereignty; let us allow that what cannot be avenged without shedding the blood of citizens was done with justice. You have seen with silent indignation, however, in past years, the treasury pillaged; you have seen kings and free people, paying tribute to a small party of Patricians, in whose hands were both the highest honors and the greatest wealth; but to have carried on such proceedings with impunity, they now deem but a small matter; and, at last, your laws and your honor, with every civil and religious obligation, have been sacrificed for the benefit of your enemies. Nor do they who have done these things show either shame or contrition, but parade proudly before your faces, displaying their sacerdotal dignities, their consulships, and some of them their triumphs, as if they regarded them as marks of honor and not as fruits of their dishonesty. Slaves, purchased with money, will not submit to unjust commands from their masters; yet you, my fellow-citizens, who were born to empire, tamely endure oppression.

But who are these, who have thus taken the government into their hands? Men of the most abandoned character, of blood-stained hands, of insatiable avarice, of enormous guilt, and of matchless pride; men by whom integrity, reputation, public spirit, and indeed everything, whether honorable or dishonorable, is converted to a means of gain. Some of them make it their defense that they have killed tribunes of the people; others, that they have instituted unjust prosecutions; others, that they have shed your blood; and thus, the more atrocities each has committed, the greater is his security; while your oppressors, whom the same desires, the same aversions, and the same fears combine in strict union (a union among good men is friendship, but among the bad is confederacy in guilt), have excited in you, through your want of spirit, that terror which they ought to feel for their own crimes.

But if your concern to preserve your liberty were as great as their ardor to increase their power of oppression, the state would not be distracted as it is at present; and the marks of favor which proceed from you would be conferred, not on the most shameless, but on the most deserving. Your forefathers, in order to assert their rights and establish their authority, twice seceded in arms to Mount Aventine; and will not you exert yourselves, to the utmost of your power, in defense of that liberty which you received from them? Will you not display so much the more spirit in the cause, from the reflection that it is a greater disgrace to lose what has been gained, than not to have gained it at all?

But some will ask me, "What course of conduct, then, would you advise us to pursue?" I would advise you to inflict punishment on those who have sacrificed the interests of their country to the enemy; not, indeed, by arms, or any violence (which would be more unbecoming, however, for you to inflict than for them to suffer), but by prosecutions, and by the evidence of Jugurtha himself, who, if he has really surrendered, will doubtless obey your summons; whereas, if he shows contempt for it, you will at once judge what sort of a peace or surrender it is from which springs impunity to Jugurtha for his crimes, immense wealth to a few men in power, and loss and infamy to the Republic.

But perhaps you are not yet weary of the tyranny of these men; perhaps these times please you less than those when kingdoms, provinces, laws, rights, the administration of justice, war, and peace, and indeed everything, civil and religious, was in the hands of an oligarchy; while you, that is, the people of Rome, though unconquered by foreign enemies and rulers of all nations around, were content with being allowed to live; for which of you had spirit to throw off your slavery? For myself, indeed, though I think it most disgraceful to receive an injury without resenting it, yet I could easily allow you to pardon these basest of traitors, because they are your fellow-citizens, were it not certain that your indulgence would end in your destruction. For such is their presumption, that to escape punishment for their misdeeds will have but little effect upon them, unless they be deprived at the same time of the power of doing mischief; and endless anxiety will remain for you if you shall have to reflect that you must either be slaves or preserve your liberty by force of arms.

Of mutual trust, or concord, what hope is there? They wish to be lords; you desire to be free; they seek to inflict injury, you to repel it; they treat your allies as enemies, your enemies as allies. With feelings so opposite, can peace or friendship subsist between you? I warn you, therefore, and exhort you, not to allow such enormous dishonesty to go unpunished. It is not an embezzlement of the public money that has been committed; nor is it a forcible extortion of money from your allies, offences which, though great, are now, from their frequency, considered as nothing; but the authority of the senate and your own power have been sacrificed to the bitterest of enemies, and the public interest has been betrayed for money, both at home and abroad; and unless these misdeeds be investigated and punishment be inflicted on the guilty, what remains for us but to live as the slaves of those who have committed them? For those who with impunity do what they will are undoubtedly kings.

I do not, however, wish to encourage you, O Romans, to be better satisfied by finding your fellow-citizens guilty than innocent, but merely to warn you not to bring ruin on the good by suffering the bad to escape. It is far better, in any government, to be unmindful of a service than of an injury; for a good man, if neglected, only becomes less active; but a bad man becomes more daring. Besides, if the crimes of the wicked are suppressed, the state will seldom need extraordinary support from the virtuous.

[Sallust's narrative:] *By repeating these and similar sentiments, Memmius prevailed on the people to send Lucius Cassius, who was then praetor, to Jugurtha, and to bring him, under guarantee of public faith, to Rome, in order that, by the prince's evidence, the misconduct of Scaurus and the rest, whom they charged with having taken bribes, might more easily be made manifest.*

SOURCE: *Sallust, Florus, and Velleius Paterculus*. Translated by John Selby Watson. London: Henry G. Bohn. 1852.

LUCIUS PHILIPPUS

AGAINST LEPIDUS (78 B.C.)

Lucius Marcius Philippus argued with the Roman senate to counter
the "turbulent" M. Aemilius Lepidus, the former consul who had
gathered an army to start a civil war to help force his reelection.
The senate was persuaded and authorized an attack on Lepidus's
army in Etruria. This oration is from one of Sallust's lost works.

I could wish, beyond all things, Conscript Fathers, that the State
should be at peace, or that, if it be in danger, it should be defended
by its ablest citizens, and that mischievous plots should prove the
ruin of their contrivers. But, on the contrary, everything is disor-
dered by factious disturbances, disturbances excited by those whom
it would better become to suppress them than to incite them. What
the worst and weakest, moreover, have determined upon, is to be
executed by the good and wise. For, though averse to your inclinations, we are to undertake war because it pleases Lepidus; unless any
of us, perchance, choose to secure him peace on our part, and to
suffer hostilities on his.

Just heaven! You, who yet rule this city, but take no thought for
its interests, behold Lepidus, the worst of all infamous characters, of
whom it cannot be decided whether his wickedness or baseness is
the greater, heads an army for the purpose of oppressing our liber-
ties, and he who was once contemptible has made himself formidable; while you, whispering and shrinking back, influenced by
words and the predictions of augurs, desire to have peace rather
than to maintain it, unmindful that, by the weakness of your

resolutions, you lessen at once your dignity and his fears. And this is a natural consequence, when, by plunder, he has gained from you a consulship, and, by his factious proceedings, a province and an army. What would he have received for good deeds, when you have bestowed such rewards on his villainies?

But, you will say, those who have voted to the last for the sending of deputies, for peace, concord, and other things of the kind, have obtained favor from him. On the contrary, they have been held in contempt, thought unworthy of any share in the administration, and fit only to be the prey of others, as persons who sue for peace with the same weakness with which they lost it when it was in their possession. For myself, when, at the very first, I saw Etruria conspiring with him, the proscribed called to his support, and the Republic rent into factions by his bribes, I thought that no time was to be lost, and accordingly followed, with a few others, the measures of Catulus. But that party which extolled the services which the Aemilian family rendered the State, and said that the greatness of the Romans had been increased by lenity, could not then perceive that Lepidus had done anything extraordinary; and even when he had taken up arms without your authority and for the destruction of your liberty, each of them, by seeking wealth and patronage for himself, weakened the public counsels. At that time, however, Lepidus was merely a marauder, at the head of a few camp-followers and cut-throats, each of whom would have periled his life for a day's wages; now he is a proconsul with full authority—an authority not bought, but conferred on him by you yourselves—and with officers still obliged by law to obey him; while there have flocked to his standard the most profligate characters of every rank, men who are turbulent from distress and cupidity and harassed with the consciousness of crimes; men who are at ease in broils and restless in peace; men who excite tumult after tumult and war after war; and men who were first the followers of Saturninus, then of Sulpicius, next of Marius and Damasippus, and have now become the instruments of Lepidus. Etruria, moreover, is in insurrection; all the embers of the last war are rekindled; the Spains are solicited to take arms; Mithridates, on the very frontier of the tributaries that still support us, is watching an opportunity to commence hostilities; and nothing but a proper leader is wanting to subvert our government.

I therefore entreat and conjure you, Conscript Fathers, to give your serious attention to this matter, and not to suffer the unbridled influence of corruption, like the ravages of a disease, to spread by contact to the uninfected. For when honors are heaped on the unprincipled, scarcely will anyone maintain an integrity which is unrewarded. Or are you waiting till, having again brought his army upon you, he attacks the city with fire and sword?—a much shorter step from his present assumptions than that from peace and concord to civil war; a war which he commenced in defiance of every obligation, human and divine; not to redress his own grievances, or those of the persons whose cause he pretends to vindicate, but to subvert our laws and our liberty. For he is disquieted and harassed with raging desires and terror for his crimes; he is undecided and restless, pursuing sometimes one scheme and sometimes another; dreading peace, and hating war; feeling that he must abstain from luxury and licentiousness, yet taking advantage meantime of your inactivity, inactivity which I do not know whether I should not rather call fear, or pusillanimity, or infatuation; for while you see peril threatening you like a thunderbolt, you merely wish, each for himself, that it may not fall upon you, but do not make the least effort to prevent it.

Consider, I pray you, how the temper of the times is changed from what it was. Formerly, designs against the Commonwealth were conducted secretly, and measures for its defense with openness, and thus the lovers of their country had a great advantage over incendiaries; now peace and concord are publicly impugned, and supported only by plans concerted in secret. Those who espouse a bad cause show themselves in arms; you, Conscript Fathers, shrink back in terror. But for what do you wait, unless you are ashamed or unwilling to act as becomes you? Do the declarations of Lepidus influence you?—of Lepidus, who says that each should have his own, and yet retains the property of others; who proclaims that laws established by arms should be abrogated, and yet seeks to bring us under his yoke by a civil war; who asserts that the civic franchise should be restored to those from whom he denies that it has been taken; and who insists, for the sake of concord, on the reestablishment of the tribunal power, by which all our discords have been inflamed.

O most abandoned and shameless of men! Have the distresses and troubles of the citizens become objects of your care, who have in your possession nothing but what has been obtained by violence and injustice? You demand a second consulship, as if you had

resigned the first; you seek a pretended peace by means of a war
that breaks the real peace which we enjoyed; you are a traitor to us,
a deceiver of your party, and the enemy of all honest men! Have
you no shame before either gods or men, both of whom you have
offended by your perfidies and perjuries? But, since you are what
you are, I exhort you to persist in your course, and to keep your
weapons in your hands; and do not make yourself uneasy, and keep
us in suspense, by delaying your traitorous purposes. Neither our
provinces, nor our laws, nor our household gods endure you as a
citizen. Proceed, then, as you have begun, that you may as soon as
possible meet your deserts!

But you, O Conscript Fathers, how long will you keep the
Republic in insecurity by your delays, and meet arms only with
words? Forces are levied against you; money is raised publicly and
privately, by extortion; troops are led out and placed in garrisons;
the laws are under arbitrary and capricious management; and yet
you, meanwhile, think only of sending deputies and preparing resolutions. But, be assured, the more earnestly you sue for peace, the
more vigorously will war be urged against you, for your enemy will
find himself better supported by your fields than by the justice and
goodness of his cause. For whoever professes a hatred of civil broils,
and of the shedding of Roman blood, and keeps you, for that reason, defenseless while Lepidus is in arms, recommends you to submit to the treatment which the vanquished must endure, when you
yourselves might inflict it on others. Such counselors advise peace
on your part towards him, and war on his towards you. If exhortations of this nature please you, if such insensibility has taken possession of your breasts that, forgetful of the crimes of Cinna, by whose
return into the city all the dignity of your order was trampled in the
dust, you will nevertheless put yourselves, your wives, your children, into the power of Lepidus, what need is there of resolutions,
or what is the use of the aid of Catulus? He, and all other honest
men, concern themselves for the State in vain.

But act as you please; the bands of Cethegus and other traitors
stand ready for you, eager to renew their ravages and burnings, and
to arm their hands afresh against our household gods. If liberty and
honor, however, have more attractions for you, decide on what is
worthy of the name of Rome, and stimulate the courage of your
valiant supporters. A new army is at your command, with colonies
of veterans, with all the nobility, and the most able commanders.

Fortune follows the braver side; and the force which the enemy has collected through our remissness will dwindle away when we begin to exert ourselves.

My opinion therefore is, since Lepidus is advancing to the gates of the city with an army, raised on his own responsibility, and with the worst enemies of the Commonwealth, and in defiance of the authority of the Senate, that Appius Claudius, the interrex, Quintus Catulus, the proconsul, and others who are in authority, shall be directed to guard the city, and *to make it their care that the Republic receive no injury.*

SOURCE: *Sallust, Florus, and Velleius Paterculus.* Translated by John Selby Watson. London: Henry G. Bohn. 1852.

CATILINE

TO THE CONSPIRATORS (63 B.C.)

In one of the most spectacular political events of the Roman Republic, L. Sergius Catilina, known to us as Catiline (108–62 B.C.), a former praetor, conspired to overthrow the government as well as murder, among others, his longtime nemesis, the orator and consul Cicero. However, Catiline portrays himself here as a hero, a revolutionary for the people: "Who in the world, indeed, that has the feelings of a man, can endure that they should have a superfluity of riches to squander in building over seas and leveling mountains, and that means should be wanting to us even for the necessaries of life; that they should join together two houses or more, and that we should not have a hearth to call our own? They, though they purchase pictures, statues, and embossed plate; though they pull down new buildings and erect others, and lavish and abuse their wealth in every possible method, yet cannot, with the utmost efforts of caprice, exhaust it. But for us there is poverty at home, debts abroad; our present circumstances are bad, our prospects much worse; and what, in a word, have we left but a miserable existence?" A deeper motivation seems to have been his disgrace at being deeply in debt; he hoped overthrowing the Roman Republic would put him in power again and free himself of financial obligations. Catiline's first address to a gathering of like-minded citizens came in a room in his own house in early November. Cicero would expose the conspiracy in the senate the next day.

If your courage and fidelity had not been sufficiently proved by me, this favorable opportunity would have occurred to no purpose; mighty hopes, absolute power, would in vain be within our grasp; nor should I, depending on irresolution or fickle-mindedness, pursue contingencies instead of certainties. But as I have, on many remarkable occasions, experienced your bravery and attachment to me, I have ventured to engage in a most important and glorious enterprise. I am aware, too, that whatever advantages or evils affect you, the same affect me; and to have the same desires and the same aversions is assuredly a firm bond of friendship.

What I have been meditating, you have already heard separately. But my ardor for action is daily more and more excited, when I consider what our future condition of life must be, unless we ourselves assert our claims to liberty. For since the government has fallen under the power and jurisdiction of a few, kings and princes have constantly been their tributaries; nations and states have paid them taxes; but all the rest of us, however brave or worthy, whether noble or plebeian, have been regarded as a mere mob, without interest or authority, and subject to those to whom, if the state were in a sound condition, we should be a terror. Hence, all influence, power, honor, and wealth, are in their hands, or where they dispose of them: to us they have left only insults, dangers, persecutions, and poverty. To such indignities, O bravest of men, how long will you submit? Is it not better to die in a glorious attempt than, after having been the sport of other men's insolence, to resign a wretched and degraded existence with ignominy?

But success (I call gods and men to witness!) is in our own hands. Our years are fresh; our spirit is unbroken: among our oppressors, on the contrary, through age and wealth a general debility has been produced. We have therefore only to make a beginning; the course of events will accomplish the rest.

Who in the world, indeed, that has the feelings of a man, can endure that they should have a superfluity of riches to squander in building over seas and leveling mountains, and that means should be wanting to us even for the necessaries of life; that they should join together two houses or more, and that we should not have a hearth to call our own? They, though they purchase pictures, statues, and embossed plate; though they pull down new buildings and erect others, and lavish and abuse their wealth in every possible method, yet cannot, with the utmost efforts of caprice, exhaust it.

But for us there is poverty at home, debts abroad; our present circumstances are bad, our prospects much worse; and what, in a word, have we left but a miserable existence?

Will you not, then, awake to action? Behold, that liberty, that liberty for which you have so often wished, with wealth, honor, and glory set before your eyes. All these prizes Fortune offers to the victorious. Let the enterprise itself, then let the opportunity, let your poverty, your dangers, and the glorious spoils of war, animate you far more than my words. Use me either as your leader or as your fellow-soldier; neither my heart nor my hand shall be wanting to you. These objects I hope to effect, in concert with you, in the character of consul; unless, indeed, my expectation deceives me, and you prefer to be slaves rather than masters.

[Sallust's narrative:] *When these men, surrounded with numberless evils, but without any resources or hopes of good, had heard this address, though they thought it much for their advantage to disturb the public tranquility, yet most of them called on Catiline to state on what terms they were to engage in the contest; what benefits they were to expect from taking up arms; and what support and encouragement they had, and in what quarters. Catiline then promised them the abolition of their debts; a proscription of the wealthy citizens; offices, sacerdotal dignities, plunder, and all other gratifications which war, and the license of conquerors, can afford. He added that Piso was in Hither Spain, and Publius Sittius Nucerinus with an army in Mauritania, both of whom were privy to his plans; that Caius Antonius, whom he hoped to have for a colleague, was canvassing for the consulship, a man with whom he was intimate, and who was involved in all manner of embarrassments; and that, in conjunction with him, he himself, when consul, would commence operations. He, moreover, assailed all the respectable citizens with reproaches, commended each of his associates by name, reminded one of his poverty, another of his ruling passion, several others of their danger or disgrace, and many of the spoils which they had obtained by the victory of Sylla. When he saw their spirits sufficiently elevated, he charged them to attend to his interest at the election of consuls, and dismissed the assembly.*

SOURCE: *Sallust, Florus, and Velleius Paterculus.* Translated by John Selby Watson. London: Henry G. Bohn. 1852.

JULIUS CAESAR

ON THE PUNISHMENT OF THE CATILINE CONSPIRATORS (63 B.C.)

When asked for his opinion by the consul during the senate debates on Catiline's conspiracy, the young Roman general Gaius Julius Caesar (100 B.C.–44 B.C.), who would become famous for his amazing military conquests and civil administration, spoke out for careful deliberation and historical reflection. "It is said," writes Plutarch, "that Caesar's natural ability as a political speaker was of the highest order, and that he took the greatest pains to cultivate it, so that in this field the second place was indisputably his. He did not aim higher than this, since his main efforts were directed towards becoming the first power in the state and the greatest soldier . . ."[1] Sallust's *Conspiracy of Catiline* provides us with this, the only recorded speech of Caesar's. (The consul Cicero's speech on this matter follows.)

It becomes all men, Conscript Fathers, who deliberate on dubious matters, to be influenced neither by hatred, affection, anger, nor pity. The mind, when such feelings obstruct its view, cannot easily see what is right; nor has any human being consulted, at the same moment, his passions and his interest. When the mind is freely exerted, its reasoning is sound; but passion, if it gain possession of it, becomes its tyrant, and reason is powerless.

---

[1] *Fall of the Roman Republic: Six Lives by Plutarch.* Translated by Rex Warner. Harmondsworth, England: Penguin. 1983. 246.

I could easily mention, Conscript Fathers, numerous examples of kings and nations, who, swayed by resentment or compassion, have adopted injudicious courses of conduct; but I had rather speak of those instances in which our ancestors, in opposition to the impulse of passion, acted with wisdom and sound policy.

In the Macedonian war, which we carried on against King Perses, the great and powerful state of Rhodes, which had risen by the aid of the Roman people, was faithless and hostile to us; yet, when the war was ended, and the conduct of the Rhodians was taken into consideration, our forefathers left them unmolested, lest any should say that war was made upon them for the sake of seizing their wealth, rather than of punishing their faithlessness. Throughout the Punic wars, too, though the Carthaginians, both during peace, and in suspensions of arms, were guilty of many acts of injustice, yet our ancestors never took occasion to retaliate, but considered rather what was worthy of themselves, than what might justly be inflicted on their enemies.

Similar caution, Conscript Fathers, is to be observed by yourselves, that the guilt of Lentulus, and the other conspirators, may not have greater weight with you than your own dignity, and that you may not regard your indignation more than your character. If, indeed, a punishment adequate to their crimes be discovered, I consent to extraordinary measures; but if the enormity of their crime exceeds whatever can be devised, I think that we should inflict only such penalties as the laws have provided.

Most of those who have given their opinions before me, have deplored, in studied and impressive language, the sad fate that threatens the republic; they have recounted the barbarities of war, and the afflictions that would fall on the vanquished; they have told us that maidens would be dishonored, and youths abused; that children would be torn from the embraces of their parents; that matrons would be subjected to the pleasure of the conquerors; that temples and dwelling-houses would be plundered; that massacres and fires would follow; and that every place would be filled with arms, corpses, blood, and lamentation. But to what end—in the name of the eternal gods—was such eloquence directed? Was it intended to render you indignant at the conspiracy? A speech, no doubt, will inflame him whom so frightful and monstrous a reality has not provoked! Far from it: for to no man does evil, directed against himself, appear a light matter; many, on the contrary, have felt it more seriously than was right.

But to different persons, Conscript Fathers, different degrees of license are allowed. If those who pass a life sunk in obscurity, commit any error, through excessive anger, few become aware of it, for their fame is as limited as their fortune; but of those who live invested with extensive power, and in an exalted station, the whole world knows the proceedings. Thus in the highest position there is the least liberty of action; and it becomes us to indulge neither partiality nor aversion, but least of all animosity; for what in others is called resentment, is in the powerful termed violence and cruelty.

I am indeed of opinion, Conscript Fathers, that the utmost degree of torture is inadequate to punish their crime; but the generality of mankind dwell on that which happens last, and, in the case of malefactors, forget their guilt, and talk only of their punishment, should that punishment have been inordinately severe. I feel assured, too, that Decimus Silanus, a man of spirit and resolution, made the suggestions which he offered, from zeal for the state, and that he had no view, in so important a matter, to favor or to enmity; such I know to be his character, and such his discretion. Yet his proposal appears to me, I will not say cruel (for what can be cruel that is directed against such characters?), but foreign to our policy. For assuredly, Silanus, either your fears, or their treason, must have induced you, a consul elect, to propose this new kind of punishment. Of fear it is unnecessary to speak, when, by the prompt activity of that distinguished man our consul, such numerous forces are under arms; and as to the punishment, we may say, what is indeed the truth, that in trouble and distress, death is a relief from suffering, and not a torment; that it puts an end to all human woes; and that beyond it, there is no place either for sorrow or joy.

But why, in the name of the immortal gods, did you not add to your proposal, Silanus, that, before they were put to death, they should be punished with the scourge? Was it because the Porcian law forbids it? But other laws forbid condemned citizens to be deprived of life, and allow them to go into exile. Or was it because scourging is a severer penalty than death? Yet what can be too severe, or too harsh, towards men convicted of such an offence? But if scourging be a milder punishment than death, how is it consistent to observe the law as to the smaller point, when you disregard it as to the greater?

But who, it may be asked, will blame any severity that shall be decreed against these parricides of their country? I answer that time, the course of events, and fortune, whose caprice governs nations, may blame it. Whatever shall fall on the traitors, will fall on them justly; but it is for you, Conscript Fathers, to consider well what you resolve to inflict on others. All precedents productive of evil effects have had their origin from what was good; but when a government passes into the hands of the ignorant or unprincipled, any new example of severity, inflicted on deserving and suitable objects, is extended to those that are improper and undeserving of it. The Lacedaemonians, when they had conquered the Athenians, appointed thirty men to govern their state. These thirty began their administration by putting to death, even without a trial, all who were notoriously wicked, or publicly detestable; acts at which the people rejoiced, and extolled their justice. But afterwards, when their lawless power gradually increased, they proceeded, at their pleasure, to kill the good and bad indiscriminately, and to strike terror into all; and thus the state, overpowered and enslaved, paid a heavy penalty for its imprudent exultation.

Within our own memory, too, when the victorious Sylla ordered Damasippus, and others of similar character, who had risen by distressing their country, to be put to death, who did not commend the proceeding? All exclaimed that wicked and factious men, who had troubled the state with their seditious practices, had justly forfeited their lives. Yet this proceeding was the commencement of great bloodshed. For whenever anyone coveted the mansion or villa, or even the plate or apparel of another, he exerted his influence to have him numbered among the proscribed. Thus they, to whom the death of Damasippus had been a subject of joy, were soon after dragged to death themselves; nor was there any cessation of slaughter, until Sylla had glutted all his partisans with riches.

Such excesses, indeed, I do not fear from Marcus Tullius, or in these times. But in a large state there arise many men of various dispositions. At some other period, and under another consul, who, like the present, may have an army at his command, some false accusation may be credited as true; and when, with our example for a precedent, the consul shall have drawn the sword on the authority of the senate, who shall stay its progress, or moderate its fury?

Our ancestors, Conscript Fathers, were never deficient in conduct or courage; nor did pride prevent them from imitating the customs of other nations, if they appeared deserving of regard. Their armor, and weapons of war, they borrowed from the Samnites; their ensigns of authority, for the most part, from the Etrurians; and, in short, whatever appeared eligible to them, whether among allies or among enemies, they adopted at home with the greatest readiness, being more inclined to emulate merit than to be jealous of it. But at the same time, adopting a practice from Greece, they punished their citizens with the scourge, and inflicted capital punishment on such as were condemned. When the republic, however, became powerful, and faction grew strong from the vast number of citizens, men began to involve the innocent in condemnation, and other like abuses were practiced; and it was then that the Porcian and other laws were provided, by which condemned citizens were allowed to go into exile.

This lenity of our ancestors, Conscript Fathers, I regard as a very strong reason why we should not adopt any new measures of severity. For assuredly there was greater merit and wisdom in those, who raised so mighty an empire from humble means, than in us, who can scarcely preserve what they so honorably acquired. Am I of opinion, then, you will ask, that the conspirators should be set free, and that the army of Catiline should thus be increased? Far from it; my recommendation is that their property be confiscated, and that they themselves be kept in custody in such of the municipal towns as are best able to bear the expense; that no one hereafter bring their case before the senate, or speak on it to the people; and that the senate now give their opinion, that he who shall act contrary to this will act against the republic and the general safety.

SOURCE: *Sallust, Florus, and Velleius Paterculus*. Translated by John Selby Watson. London: Henry G. Bohn. 1852.

CICERO

THE FIRST ORATION AGAINST CATILINE (63 B.C.)

The most renowned orator in the Western world, Marcus Tullius Cicero (106–43 B.C.) was a writer, lawyer and politician; his tone, unlike those of the great Greek orators, is personal and conversational, joky and prosecutorial. At the time of Catiline's conspiracy against the Roman Republic, he was one of two consuls, the elected heads of the republic. He detected the conspiracy (he explains how, below) and in the midst of this most famous of courtroom dramas lambasts Catiline's character, forever coloring the world's understanding of the conspirator. "For Cicero, it may be said, was the one man, above all others," wrote Plutarch, "who made the Romans feel how great a charm eloquence lends to what is good, and how invincible justice is, if it be well spoken; and that it is necessary for him who would dexterously govern a commonwealth, in action, always to prefer that which is honest before that which is popular, and in speaking, to free the right and useful measure from everything that may occasion offence."[1] Catiline's speech to his army in early 62 B.C. follows this oration.

When, O Catiline, do you mean to cease abusing our patience? How long is that madness of yours still to mock us? When is there

---

[1] *The Lives of the Nobel Grecians and Romans.* Translated by John Dryden. Revised by Arthur Hugh Clough. New York: Modern Library (Random House). 1932. 1048.

to be an end of that unbridled audacity of yours, swaggering about as it does now? Do not the nightly guards placed on the Palatine Hill—do not the watches posted throughout the city—does not the alarm of the people, and the union of all good men—does not the precaution taken of assembling the senate in this most defensible place—do not the looks and countenances of this venerable body here present, have any effect upon you? Do you not feel that your plans are detected? Do you not see that your conspiracy is already arrested and rendered powerless by the knowledge which everyone here possesses of it? What is there that you did last night, what the night before—where is it that you were—who was there that you summoned to meet you—what design was there which was adopted by you, with which you think that any one of us is unacquainted?

Shame on the age and on its principles! The senate is aware of these things; the consul sees them; and yet this man lives. Lives! Aye, he comes even into the senate. He takes a part in the public deliberations; he is watching and marking down and checking off for slaughter every individual among us. And we, gallant men that we are, think that we are doing our duty to the republic if we keep out of the way of his frenzied attacks.

You ought, O Catiline, long ago to have been led to execution by command of the consul. That destruction which you have been long plotting against us ought to have already fallen on your own head.

What? Did not that most illustrious man, Publius Scipio, the Pontifex Maximus, in his capacity of a private citizen, put to death Tiberius Gracchus, though but slightly undermining the constitution? And shall we, who are the consuls, tolerate Catiline, openly desirous to destroy the whole world with fire and slaughter? For I pass over older instances, such as how Caius Servilius Ahala with his own hand slew Spurius Maelius when plotting a revolution in the state. There was—there was once such virtue in this republic that brave men would repress mischievous citizens with severer chastisement than the most bitter enemy. For we have a resolution of the senate, a formidable and authoritative decree against you, O Catiline; the wisdom of the republic is not at fault, nor the dignity of this senatorial body. We, we alone—I say it openly,—we, the consuls, are wanting in our duty.

The senate once passed a decree that Lucius Opimius, the consul, should take care that the republic suffered no injury. Not one night elapsed. There was put to death, on some mere suspicion of disaffection, Caius Gracchus, a man whose family had borne the most unblemished reputation for many generations. There was slain Marcus Fulvius, a man of consular rank, and all his children. By a like decree of the senate the safety of the republic was entrusted to Caius Marius and Lucius Valerius, the consuls. Did not the vengeance of the republic, did not execution overtake Lucius Saturninus, a tribune of the people, and Caius Servilius, the praetor, without the delay of one single day? But we, for these twenty days, have been allowing the edge of the senate's authority to grow blunt, as it were. For we are in possession of a similar decree of the senate, but we keep it locked up in its parchment—buried, I may say, in the sheath; and according to this decree you ought, O Catiline, to be put to death this instant. You live,—and you live, not to lay aside, but to persist in your audacity.

I wish, O conscript fathers, to be merciful; I wish not to appear negligent amid such danger to the state; but I do now accuse myself of remissness and culpable inactivity. A camp is pitched in Italy, at the entrance of Etruria, in hostility to the republic; the number of the enemy increases every day; and yet the general of that camp, the leader of those enemies, we see within the walls—aye, and even in the senate—planning every day some internal injury to the republic. If, O Catiline, I should now order you to be arrested, to be put to death, I should, I suppose, have to fear lest all good men should say that I had acted tardily, rather than that anyone should affirm that I acted cruelly. But yet this, which ought to have been done long since, I have good reason for not doing as yet; I will put you to death, then, when there shall be not one person possible to be found so wicked, so abandoned, so like yourself, as not to allow that it has been rightly done. As long as one person exists who can dare to defend you, you shall live; but you shall live as you do now, surrounded by my many and trusty guards, so that you shall not be able to stir one finger against the republic; many eyes and ears shall still observe and watch you, as they have hitherto done, though you shall not perceive them.

For what is there, O Catiline, that you can still expect, if night is not able to veil your nefarious meetings in darkness, and if private houses cannot conceal the voice of your conspiracy within their walls—if everything is seen and displayed? Change your mind: trust me: forget the slaughter and conflagration you are meditating. You are hemmed in on all sides; all your plans are clearer than the day to us; let me remind you of them. Do you recollect that on the 21st of October I said in the senate that on a certain day, which was to be the 27th of October, C. Manlius, the satellite and servant of your audacity, would be in arms? Was I mistaken, Catiline, not only in so important, so atrocious, so incredible a fact, but, what is much more remarkable, in the very day? I said also in the senate that you had fixed the massacre of the nobles for the 28th of October when many chief men of the senate had left Rome, not so much for the sake of saving themselves as of checking your designs. Can you deny that on that very day you were so hemmed in by my guards and my vigilance that you were unable to stir one finger against the republic; when you said that you would be content with the flight of the rest, and the slaughter of us who remained? What? When you made sure that you would be able to seize Praeneste on the 1st of November by a nocturnal attack, did you not find that that colony was fortified by my order, by my garrison, by my watchfulness and care? You do nothing, you plan nothing, you think of nothing which I not only do not hear, but which I do not see and know every particular of.

Listen while I speak of the night before. You shall now see that I watch far more actively for the safety than you do for the destruction of the republic. I say that you came the night before (I will say nothing obscurely) into the Scythe-dealers' Street, to the house of Marcus Lecca; that many of your accomplices in the same insanity and wickedness came there, too. Do you dare to deny it? Why are you silent? I will prove it if you do deny it; for I see here in the senate some men who were there with you.

O ye immortal gods, where on earth are we? In what city are we living? What constitution is ours? There are here,—here in our body, O conscript fathers, in this the most holy and dignified assembly of the whole world, men who meditate my death, and the death of all of us, and the destruction of this city, and of the whole world. I, the consul, see them; I ask them their opinion about the republic, and I do not yet attack, even by words, those who ought to be put to death by the sword. You were, then, O Catiline, at Lecca's that night; you divided Italy into sections; you settled where everyone was to go; you fixed whom you were to leave at Rome, whom you were to take with you; you portioned out the divisions of the city for conflagration; you undertook that you yourself

would at once leave the city, and said that there was then only this
to delay you,—that I was still alive. Two Roman knights were
found to deliver you from this anxiety, and to promise that very
night, before daybreak, to slay me in my bed. All this I knew almost
before your meeting had broken up. I strengthened and fortified
my house with a stronger guard; I refused admittance, when they
came, to those whom you sent in the morning to salute me, and of
whom I had foretold to many eminent men that they would come
to me at that time.

As, then, this is the case, O Catiline, continue as you have
begun. Leave the city at least; the gates are open; depart. That
Manlian camp of yours has been waiting too long for you as its
general. And lead forth with you all your friends, or at least as many
as you can; purge the city of your presence; you will deliver me
from a great fear, when there is a wall between you and me.
Among us you can dwell no longer—I will not bear it, I will not
permit it, I will not tolerate it. Great thanks are due to the immortal
gods, and to this very Jupiter Stator, in whose temple we are, the
most ancient protector of this city, that we have already so often
escaped so foul, so horrible, and so deadly an enemy to the republic. But the safety of the commonwealth must not be too often
allowed to be risked on one man. As long as you, O Catiline, plot-
ted against me while I was the consul-elect, I defended myself, not
with a public guard, but by my own private diligence. When, in
the next consular comitia, you wished to slay me when I was actually consul, and your competitors also, in the Campus Martius, I
checked your nefarious attempt by the assistance and resources of
my own friends, without exciting any disturbance publicly. In
short, as often as you attacked me, I by myself opposed you, and
that, too, though I saw that my ruin was connected with great
disaster to the republic. But now you are openly attacking the
entire republic.

You are summoning to destruction and devastation the temples
of the immortal gods, the houses of the city, the lives of all the citizens—in short, all Italy. Wherefore, since I do not yet venture to
do that which is the best thing, and which belongs to my office and
to the discipline of our ancestors, I will do that which is more merciful if we regard its rigor, and more expedient for the State. For if
I order you to be put to death, the rest of the conspirators will still
remain in the republic; if, as I have long been exhorting you, you

depart, your companions, those worthless dregs of the republic, will be drawn off from the city, too. What is the matter, Catiline? Do you hesitate to do that when I order you which you were already doing of your own accord? The consul orders an enemy to depart from the city. Do you ask me, Are you to go into banishment? I do not order it; but, if you consult me, I advise it.

For what is there, O Catiline, that can now afford you any pleasure in this city? For there is no one in it, except that band of profligate conspirators of yours, who does not fear you,—no one who does not hate you. What brand of domestic baseness is not stamped upon your life? What disgraceful circumstance is wanting to your infamy in your private affairs? From what licentiousness have your eyes, from what atrocity have your hands, from what iniquity has your whole body ever abstained? Is there one youth, when you have once entangled him in the temptations of your corruption, to whom you have not held out a sword for audacious crime, or a torch for licentious wickedness?

What? When lately by the death of your former wife you had made your house empty and ready for a new bridal, did you not even add another incredible wickedness to this wickedness? But I pass that over, and willingly allow it to be buried in silence, that so horrible a crime may not be seen to have existed in this city, and not to have been chastised. I pass over the ruin of your fortune, which you know is hanging over you against the ides of the very next month; I come to those things which relate not to the infamy of your private vices, not to your domestic difficulties and baseness, but to the welfare of the republic and to the lives and safety of us all.

Can the light of this life, O Catiline, can the breath of this atmosphere be pleasant to you, when you know that there is not one man of those here present who is ignorant that you, on the last day of the year, when Lepidus and Tullus were consuls, stood in the assembly armed; that you had prepared your hand for the slaughter of the consuls and chief men of the state, and that no reason or fear of yours hindered your crime and madness, but the fortune of the republic? And I say no more of these things, for they are not unknown to everyone. How often have you endeavored to slay me, both as consul-elect and as actual consul? How many shots of yours, so aimed that they seemed impossible to be escaped, have I avoided by some slight stooping aside, and some dodging, as it were, of my body? You attempt nothing, you execute nothing, you devise nothing that can be kept hid from me at the proper time; and yet you do not cease to attempt and to contrive. How often already has that dagger of yours been wrested from your hands? How often has it slipped through them by some chance, and dropped down? And yet you cannot any longer do without it; and to what sacred mysteries it is consecrated and devoted by you I know not, that you think it necessary to plunge it in the body of the consul.

But now, what is that life of yours that you are leading? For I will speak to you not so as to seem influenced by the hatred I ought to feel, but by pity, nothing of which is due to you. You came a little while ago into the senate; in so numerous an assembly, who of so many friends and connections of yours saluted you? If this in the memory of man never happened to anyone else, are you waiting for insults by word of mouth, when you are overwhelmed by the most irresistible condemnation of silence? Is it nothing that at your arrival all those seats were vacated, that all the men of consular rank, who had often been marked out by you for slaughter, the very moment you sat down, left that part of the benches bare and vacant? With what feelings do you think you ought to bear this? On my honor, if my slaves feared me as all your fellow citizens fear you, I should think I must leave my house. Do not you think you should leave the city?

If I say that I was even undeservedly so suspected and hated by my fellow citizens, I would rather flee from their sight than be gazed at by the hostile eyes of everyone. And do you, who, from the consciousness of your wickedness, know that the hatred of all men is just and has been long due to you, hesitate to avoid the sight and presence of those men whose minds and senses you offend? If your parents feared and hated you, and if you could by no means pacify them, you would, I think, depart somewhere out of their sight. Now, your country, which is the common parent of all of us, hates and fears you, and has no other opinion of you, than that you are meditating parricide in her case; and will you neither feel awe of her authority, nor deference for her judgment, nor fear of her power?

And she, O Catiline, thus pleads with you, and after a manner silently speaks to you: There has now for many years been no crime committed but by you; no atrocity has taken place without you;

you alone unpunished and unquestioned have murdered the citizens, have harassed and plundered the allies; you alone have had power not only to neglect all laws and investigations, but to overthrow and break through them. Your former actions, though they ought not to have been borne, yet I did bear as well as I could; but now that I should be wholly occupied with fear of you alone, that at every sound I should dread Catiline, that no design should seem possible to be entertained against me which does not proceed from your wickedness, this is no longer endurable. Depart, then, and deliver me from this fear—that, if it be a just one, I may not be destroyed; if an imaginary one, that at least I may at last cease to fear.

If, as I have said, your country were thus to address you, ought she not to obtain her request, even if she were not able to enforce it? What shall I say of your having given yourself into custody? What of your having said, for the sake of avoiding suspicion, that you were willing to dwell in the house of Marcus Lepidus? And when you were not received by him, you dared even to come to me, and begged me to keep you in my house; and when you had received answer from me that I could not possibly be safe in the same house with you, when I considered myself in great danger as long as we were in the same city, you came to Quintus Metellus, the praetor, and being rejected by him, you passed on to your associate, that most excellent man, Marcus Marcellus, who would be, I suppose you thought, most diligent in guarding you, most sagacious in suspecting you, and most bold in punishing you; but how far can we think that man ought to be from bonds and imprisonment who has already judged himself deserving of being given into custody.

Since, then, this is the case, do you hesitate, O Catiline, if you cannot remain here with tranquility, to depart to some distant land, and to trust your life, saved from just and deserved punishment, to flight and solitude? Make a motion, say you, to the senate (for that is what you demand), and if this body votes that you ought to go into banishment, you say that you will obey. I will not make such a motion—it is contrary to my principles, and yet I will let you see what these men think of you. Be gone from the city, O Catiline; deliver the republic from fear; depart into banishment, if that is the word you are waiting for. What now, O Catiline? Do you not perceive, do you not see the silence of these men; they permit it, they say nothing; why wait you for the authority of their words when you see their wishes in their silence?

But had I said the same to this excellent young man, Publius Sextius, or to that brave man, Marcus Marcellus, before this time the senate would deservedly have laid violent hands on me, consul though I be, in this very temple. But as to you, Catiline, while they are quiet they approve, while they permit me to speak they vote, while they are silent they are loud and eloquent. And not they alone, whose authority forsooth is dear to you, though their lives are unimportant, but the Roman knights, too, those most honorable and excellent men, and the other virtuous citizens who are now surrounding the senate, whose numbers you could see, whose desires you could know, and whose voices you a few minutes ago could hear,—aye, whose very hands and weapons I have for some time been scarcely able to keep off from you; but those, too, I will easily bring to attend you to the gates if you leave these places you have been long desiring to lay waste.

And yet, why am I speaking? That anything may change your purpose? That you may ever amend your life? That you may meditate flight or think of voluntary banishment? I wish the gods may give you such a mind; though I see, if alarmed at my words you bring your mind to go into banishment, what a storm of unpopularity hangs over me, if not at present, while the memory of your wickedness is fresh, at all events hereafter. But it is worth while to incur that, as long as that is but a private misfortune of my own, and is unconnected with the dangers of the republic. But we cannot expect that you should be concerned at your own vices, that you should fear the penalties of the laws, or that you should yield to the necessities of the republic, for you are not, O Catiline, one whom either shame can recall from infamy, or fear from danger, or reason from madness.

Wherefore, as I have said before, go forth, and if you wish to make me your enemy, as you call me, unpopular, go straight into banishment. I shall scarcely be able to endure all that will be said if you do so; I shall scarcely be able to support my load of unpopularity if you do go into banishment at the command of the consul; but if you wish to serve my credit and reputation, go forth with your ill-omened band of profligates; betake yourself to Manlius, rouse up the abandoned citizens, separate yourself from the good ones, wage war against your country, exult in your impious banditti, so that you may not seem to have been driven out by me and gone to strangers, but to have gone invited to your own friends.

Though why should I invite you, by whom I know men have been already sent on to wait in arms for you at the forum Aurelium; who I know has fixed and agreed with Manlius upon a settled day; by whom I know that that silver eagle, which I trust will be ruinous and fatal to you and to all your friends, and to which there was set up in your house a shrine as it were of your crimes, has been already sent forward. Need I fear that you can long do without that which you used to worship when going out to murder, and from whose altars you have often transferred your impious hand to the slaughter of citizens?

You will go at last where your unbridled and mad desire has been long hurrying you. And this causes you no grief, but an incredible pleasure. Nature has formed you, desire has trained you, fortune has preserved you for this insanity. Not only did you never desire quiet, but you never even desired any war but a criminal one; you have collected a band of profligates and worthless men, abandoned not only by all fortune but even by hope.

Then what happiness will you enjoy! With what delight will you exult! In what pleasure will you revel! When in so numerous a body of friends, you neither hear nor see one good man. All the toils you have gone through have always pointed to this sort of life; your lying on the ground not merely to lie in wait to gratify your unclean desires, but even to accomplish crimes; your vigilance, not only when plotting against the sleep of husbands, but also against the goods of your murdered victims, have all been preparations for this. Now you have an opportunity of displaying your splendid endurance of hunger, of cold, of want of everything; by which in a short time you will find yourself worn out. All this I effected when I procured your rejection from the consulship, that you should be reduced to make attempts on your country as an exile, instead of being able to distress it as consul, and that that which had been wickedly undertaken by you should be called piracy rather than war.

Now that I may remove and avert, O conscript fathers, any in the least reasonable complaint from myself, listen, I beseech you, carefully to what I say, and lay it up in your inmost hearts and minds. In truth, if my country, which is far dearer to me than my life—if all Italy—if the whole republic were to address me, "Marcus Tullius, what are you doing? Will you permit that man to depart whom you have ascertained to be an enemy? Whom you see ready to become the general of the war? Whom you know to be expected in the camp of the enemy as their chief, the author of all this wickedness, the head of the conspiracy, the instigator of the slaves and abandoned citizens, so that he shall seem not driven out of the city by you, but let loose by you against the city? Will you not order him to be thrown into prison, to be hurried off to execution, to be put to death with the most prompt severity? What hinders you? Is it the customs of our ancestors? But even private men have often in this republic slain mischievous citizens. Is it the laws which have been passed about the punishment of Roman citizens? But in this city those who have rebelled against the republic have never had the rights of citizens. Do you fear odium with posterity? You are showing fine gratitude to the Roman people which has raised you, a man known only by your own actions, of no ancestral renown, through all the degrees of honor at so early an age to the very highest office, if from fear of unpopularity or of any danger you neglect the safety of your fellow citizens. But if you have a fear of unpopularity, is that arising from the imputation of vigor and boldness, or that arising from that of inactivity and indecision most to be feared? When Italy is laid waste by war, when cities are attacked and houses in flames, do you not think that you will be then consumed by a perfect conflagration of hatred?"

To this holy address of the republic, and to the feelings of those men who entertain the same opinion, I will make this short answer: If, O conscript fathers, I thought it best that Catiline should be punished with death, I would not have given the space of one hour to this gladiator to live in. If, forsooth, those excellent men and most illustrious cities not only did not pollute themselves, but even glorified themselves by the blood of Saturninus, and the Gracchi, and Flaccus, and many others of old time, surely I had no cause to fear lest for slaying this parricidal murderer of the citizens any unpopularity should accrue to me with posterity. And if it did threaten me to ever so great a degree, yet I have always been of the disposition to think unpopularity earned by virtue and glory not unpopularity.

Though there are some men in this body who either do not see what threatens, or dissemble what they do see; who have fed the hope of Catiline by mild sentiments, and have strengthened the rising conspiracy by not believing it; influenced by whose authority many, and they not wicked, but only ignorant, if I punished him would say that I had acted cruelly and tyrannically. But I know that if he arrives at the camp of Manlius to which he is going, there will be no one so stupid as not to see that there has been a conspiracy, no one so hardened as not to confess it. But if this man alone were put to death, I know that this disease of the republic would be only checked for a while, not eradicated forever. But if he banishes himself, and takes with him all his friends, and collects at one point all the ruined men from every quarter, then not only will this full-grown plague of the republic be extinguished and eradicated, but also the root and seed of all future evils.

We have now for a long time, O conscript fathers, lived among these dangers and machinations of conspiracy; but somehow or other, the ripeness of all wickedness, and of this long-standing madness and audacity, has come to a head at the time of my consulship. But if this man alone is removed from this piratical crew, we may appear, perhaps, for a short time relieved from fear and anxiety, but the danger will settle down and lie hid in the veins and bowels of the republic. As it often happens that men afflicted with a severe disease, when they are tortured with heat and fever, if they drink cold water, seem at first to be relieved, but afterward suffer more and more severely; so this disease which is in the republic, if relieved by the punishment of this man, will only get worse and worse, as the rest will be still alive.

Wherefore, O conscript fathers, let the worthless be gone,—let them separate themselves from the good,—let them collect in one place,—let them, as I have often said before, be separated from us by a wall; let them cease to plot against the consul in his own house,—to surround the tribunal of the city praetor,—to besiege the senate-house with swords,—to prepare brands and torches to burn the city; let it, in short, be written on the brow of every citizen, what his sentiments are about the republic. I promise you, this, O conscript fathers, that there shall be so much diligence in us the consuls, so much authority in you, so much virtue in the Roman knights, so much unanimity in all good men that you shall see everything made plain and manifest by the departure of Catiline,— everything checked and punished.

With these omens, O Catiline, be gone to your impious and nefarious war, to the great safety of the republic, to your own misfortune and injury, and to the destruction of those who have joined themselves to you in every wickedness and atrocity. Then do you,

O Jupiter, who were consecrated by Romulus with the same auspices as this city, whom we rightly call the stay of this city and empire, repel this man and his companions from your altars and from the other temples,—from the houses and walls of the city,—from the lives and fortunes of all the citizens; and overwhelm all the enemies of good men, the foes of the republic, the robbers of Italy, men bound together by a treaty and infamous alliance of crimes, dead and alive, with eternal punishments.

SOURCE: *The Orations of Marcus Tullius Cicero.* Translated by C. D. Yonge. London: Henry G. Bohn. 1852.

CATILINE

TO HIS SOLDIERS (62 B.C.)

Lucius Sergius Catilina (known to us as Catiline) and his hopes for a revolution in the Roman Republic failed (see his "To the Conspirators" above), but in early January, as he led his army away from Rome, he tried to rally his men. Later, as the historian Sallust narrates it, "when he saw his army routed, and himself left with but few supporters, remembering his birth and former dignity, [Catiline] rushed into the thickest of the enemy, where he was slain, fighting to the last."

———◆———

[Sallust's narrative:] *When Catiline saw that he was surrounded by mountains and by hostile forces, that his schemes in the city had been unsuccessful, and that there was no hope either of escape or of succor, thinking it best, in such circumstances, to try the fortune of a battle, he resolved upon engaging, as speedily as possible, with Antonius. Having, therefore, assembled his troops, he addressed them in the following words:*

I am well aware, soldiers, that words cannot inspire courage; and that a spiritless army cannot be rendered active, or a timid army valiant, by the speech of its commander. Whatever courage is in the heart of a man, whether from nature or from habit, so much will be shown by him in the field; and on him whom neither glory nor danger can move, exhortation is bestowed in vain; for the terror in his breast stops his ears.

I have called you together, however, to give you a few instructions, and to explain to you, at the same time, my reasons for the

155

course which I have adopted. You all know, soldiers, how severe a
penalty the inactivity and cowardice of Lentulus has brought upon
himself and us; and how, while waiting for reinforcements from the
city, I was unable to march into Gaul. In what situation our affairs
now are, you all understand as well as I myself. Two armies of the
enemy, one on the side of Rome, and the other on that of Gaul,
oppose our progress; while the want of corn and of other necessaries prevents us from remaining, however strongly we may desire to
remain in our present position. Whithersoever we would go, we
must open a passage with our swords.

I conjure you, therefore, to maintain a brave and resolute spirit;
and to remember, when you advance to battle, that on your own
right hands depend riches, honor, and glory, with the enjoyment
of your liberty and of your country. If we conquer, all will be safe;
we shall have provisions in abundance, and the colonies and cor-
porate towns will open their gates to us. But if we lose the victory
through want of courage, those same places will turn against us;
for neither place nor friend will protect him whom his arms have
not protected. Besides, soldiers, the exigency does not press upon
our adversaries as presses upon us; we fight for our country, for
our liberty, for our life; they contend for what little concerns
them, the power of a small party. Attack them, therefore, with so
much the greater confidence, and call to mind your achievements
of old.

We might, with the utmost ignominy, have passed the rest of our
days in exile. Some of you, after losing your property, might have
waited at Rome for assistance from others. But because such a life,
to men of spirit, was disgusting and unendurable, you resolved
upon your present course. If you wish to quit it, you must exert all
your resolution, for none but conquerors have exchanged war for
peace. To hope for safety in flight, when you have turned away
from the enemy the arms by which the body is defended, is indeed
madness. In battle, those who are most afraid are always in most
danger; while courage is equivalent to a rampart.

When I contemplate you, soldiers, and when I consider your past
exploits, a strong hope of victory animates me. Your spirit, your
age, your valor, give me confidence; to say nothing of necessity,
which makes even cowards brave. To prevent the numbers of the
enemy from surrounding us, our confined situation is sufficient.
But should Fortune be unjust to your valor, take care not to lose

your lives unavenged; take care not to be taken and butchered like cattle, rather than, fighting like men, leave to your enemies a bloody and mournful victory.

SOURCE: *Sallust, Florus, and Velleius Paterculus*. Translated by John Selby Watson. London: Henry G. Bohn. 1852.

CICERO

THE FOURTH PHILIPPIC (44 B.C.)

Cicero delivered this speech to the people in the forum, after having addressed the senate. Cicero named this series of his speeches "Philippics" after those of the Greek orator Demosthenes (who in his series of speeches had been rallying Athens to be wary of Philip, King of Macedon); Cicero's target was Mark Antony (Marcus Antonius), the consul of the republic. In 43 B.C., Cicero was assassinated; Antony had the corpse beheaded and its hands (responsible for these Philippics) cut off.

————◆————

The great numbers in which you are here met this day, O Romans, and this assembly, greater than, it seems to me, I ever remember, inspires me with both an exceeding eagerness to defend the republic, and with a great hope of reestablishing it. Although my courage indeed has never failed; what has been unfavorable is the time; and the moment that that has appeared to show any dawn of light, I at once have been the leader in the defense of your liberty. And if I had attempted to have done so before, I should not be able to do so now. For this day, O Romans (that you may not think it is but a trifling business in which we have been engaged), the foundations have been laid for future actions. For the senate has no longer been content with styling Antonius an enemy in words, but it has shown by actions that it thinks him one. And now I am much more elated still, because you too with such great unanimity and with such a clamor have sanctioned our declaration that he is an enemy.

And indeed, O Romans, it is impossible but that either the men must be impious who have levied armies against the consul, or else that he must be an enemy against whom they have rightly taken arms. And this doubt the senate has this day removed not indeed that there really was any; but it has prevented the possibility of there being any. Caius Caesar, who has upheld and who is still upholding the republic and your freedom by his zeal and wisdom, and at the expense of his patrimonial estate, has been complimented with the highest praises of the senate.

I praise you, yes, I praise you greatly, O Romans, when you follow with the most grateful minds the name of that most illustrious youth, or rather boy; for his actions belong to immortality, the name of youth only to his age. I can recollect many things; I have heard of many things; I have read of many things; but in the whole history of the whole world I have never known anything like this. For, when we were weighed down with slavery, when the evil was daily increasing, when we had no defense, while we were in dread of the pernicious and fatal return of Marcus Antonius from Brundusium, this young man adopted the design which none of us had ventured to hope for, which beyond all question none of us were acquainted with, of raising an invincible army of his father's soldiers, and so hindering the frenzy of Antonius, spurred on as it was by the most inhuman counsels, from the power of doing mischief to the republic.

For who is there who does not see clearly that, if Caesar had not prepared an army, the return of Antonius must have been accompanied by our destruction? For, in truth, he returned in such a state of mind, burning with hatred of you all, stained with the blood of the Roman citizens, whom he had murdered at Suessa and at Brundusium, that he thought of nothing but the utter destruction of the republic. And what protection could have been found for your safety and for your liberty if the army of Caius Caesar had not been composed of the bravest of his father's soldiers? And with respect to his praises and honors, and he is entitled to divine and everlasting honors for his godlike and undying services, the senate has just consented to my proposals, and has decreed that a motion be submitted to it at the very earliest opportunity.

Now who is there who does not see that by this decree Antonius has been adjudged to be an enemy? For what else can we call him, when the senate decides that extraordinary honors are to be devised for those men who are leading armies against him? What, did not the Martial legion (which appears to me by some divine permission to have derived its name from that god from whom we have heard that the Roman people descended) decide by its resolutions that Antonius was an enemy before the senate had come to any resolution? For if he be not an enemy, we must inevitably decide that those men who have deserted the consul are enemies.

Admirably and seasonably, O Romans, have you by your cries sanctioned the noble conduct of the men of the Martial legion, who have come over to the authority of the senate, to your liberty, and to the whole republic; and have abandoned that enemy and robber and parricide of his country. Nor did they display only their spirit and courage in doing this, but their caution and wisdom also. They encamped at Alba, in a city convenient, fortified, near, full of brave men and loyal and virtuous citizens. The fourth legion imitating the virtue of this Martial legion, under the leadership of Lucius. Egnatuleius, whom the senate deservedly praised a little while ago, has also joined the army of Caius Caesar.

What more adverse decisions, O Marcus Antonius, can you want? Caesar, who has levied an army against you, is extolled to the skies. The legions are praised in the most complimentary language, which have abandoned you, which were sent for into Italy by you; and which, if you had chosen to be a consul rather than an enemy, were wholly devoted to you. And the fearless and honest decision of those legions is confirmed by the senate, is approved of by the whole Roman people, unless, indeed, you today, O Romans, decide that Antonius is a consul and not an enemy. I thought, O Romans, that you did think as you show you do. What do you suppose that the municipal towns, and the colonies, and the prefectures have any other opinion? All men are agreed with one mind; so that everyone who wishes the state to be saved must take up every sort of arms against that pestilence. I should like to know what does the opinion of Decimus Brutus, O Romans, which you can gather from his edict, which has this day reached us, appear to anyone deserving of being lightly esteemed? Rightly and truly do you say No, O Romans. For the family and name of Brutus has been by some especial kindness and liberality of the immortal gods given to the republic, for the purpose of at one time establishing, and at another of recovering, the liberty of the Roman people.

What then has been the opinion which Decimus Brutus has formed of Marcus Antonius? He excludes him from his province. He opposes him with his army. He rouses all Gaul to war, which is already roused of its own accord, and in consequence of the judgment which it has itself formed. If Antonius be consul, Brutus is an enemy. Can we then doubt which of these alternatives is the fact?

And just as you now with one mind and one voice affirm that you entertain no doubt, so did the senate just now decree that Decimus Brutus deserved excellently well of the republic, inasmuch as he was defending the authority of the senate and the liberty and empire of the Roman people. Defending it against whom? Why, against an enemy. For what other sort of defense deserves praise? In the next place the province of Gaul is praised, and is deservedly complimented in most honorable language by the senate for resisting Antonius. But if that province considered him the consul, and still refused to receive him, it would be guilty of great wickedness. For all the provinces belong to the consul of right, and are bound to obey him.

Decimus Brutus, imperator and consul elect, a citizen born for the republic, denies that he is consul; Gaul denies it; all Italy denies it; the senate denies it; you deny it. Who then thinks that he is consul except a few robbers? Although even they themselves do not believe what they say; nor is it possible that they should differ from the judgment of all men, impious and desperate men though they be. But the hope of plunder and booty blinds their minds—men whom no gifts of money, no allotment of land nor even that interminable auction has satisfied; who have proposed to themselves the city, the properties and fortunes of all the citizens as their booty; and who, as long as there is something for them to seize and carry off, think that nothing will be wanting to them; among whom Marcus Antonius (O ye immortal gods, avert, I pray you, and efface this omen), has promised to divide this city.

May things rather happen, O Romans, as you pray that they should, and may the chastisement of this frenzy fall on him and on his friend. And, indeed, I feel sure that it will be so. For I think that at present not only men but the immortal gods have all united together to preserve this republic. For if the immortal gods foreshow us the future, by means of portents and prodigies, then it has been openly revealed to us that punishment is near at hand to him, and liberty to us. Or if it was impossible for such unanimity on the part of all men to exist without the inspiration of the gods, in either case how can we doubt as to the indications of the heavenly deities? It only remains, O Romans, for you to persevere in the sentiments which you at present display.

I will act, therefore, as commanders are in the habit of doing when their army is ready for battle, who, although they see their soldiers ready to engage, still address an exhortation to them; and in like manner I will exhort you who are already eager and burning to recover your liberty. You have not, indeed, O Romans, to war against an enemy with whom it is possible to make peace on any terms whatever. For he does not now desire your slavery, as he did before, but he is angry now and thirsts for your blood. No sport appears more delightful to him than bloodshed, and slaughter, and the massacre of citizens before his eyes.

You have not, O Romans, to deal with a wicked and profligate man, but with an unnatural and savage beast. And, since he has fallen into a well, let him be buried in it. For if he escapes out of it, there will be no inhumanity of torture which it will be possible to avoid. But he is at present hemmed in, pressed, and besieged by those troops which we already have, and will soon be still more so by those which in a few days the new consuls will levy. Apply yourselves then to this business, as you are doing. Never have you shown greater unanimity in any cause; never have you been so cordially united with the senate. And no wonder. For the question now is not in what condition we are to live, but whether we are to live at all, or to perish with torture and ignominy.

Although nature, indeed, has appointed death for all men: but valor is accustomed to ward off any cruelty or disgrace in death. And that is an inalienable possession of the Roman race and name. Preserve, I beseech you, O Romans, this attribute which your ancestors have left you as a sort of inheritance. Although all other things are uncertain, fleeting, transitory; virtue alone is planted firm with very deep roots; it cannot be undermined by any violence; it can never be moved from its position. By it your ancestors first subdued the whole of Italy; then destroyed Carthage, overthrew Numantia, and reduced the most mighty kings and most warlike nations under the dominion of this empire.

And your ancestors, O Romans, had to deal with an enemy who had also a republic, a senate-house, a treasury, harmonious and united citizens, and with whom, if fortune had so willed it, there might have been peace and treaties on settled principles. But this enemy of yours is attacking your republic, but has none himself; is eager to destroy the senate, that is to say, the council of the whole world, but has no public council himself; he has exhausted your treasury, and has none of his own. For how can a man be supported by the unanimity of his citizens, who has no city at all? And what principles of peace can there be with that man who is full of incredible cruelty, and destitute of faith?

The whole then of the contest, O Romans, which is now before the Roman people, the conqueror of all nations, is with an assassin, a robber, a Spartacus. For as to his habitual boast of being like Catiline, he is equal to him in wickedness, but inferior in energy. He, though he had no army, rapidly levied one. This man has lost that very army which he had. As, therefore, by my diligence, and the authority of the senate, and your own zeal and valor, you crushed Catiline, so you will very soon hear that this infamous piratical enterprise of Antonius has been put down by your own perfect and unexampled harmony with the senate, and by the good fortune and valor of your armies and generals.

I, for my part, as far as I am able to labor, and to effect anything by my care, and exertions, and vigilance, and authority, and counsel, will omit nothing which I may think serviceable to your liberty. Nor could I omit it without wickedness after all your most ample and honorable kindness to me. However, on this day, encouraged by the motion of a most gallant man, and one most firmly attached to you, Marcus Servilius, whom you see before you, and his colleagues also, most distinguished men, and most virtuous citizens; and partly, too, by my advice and my example, we have, for the first time after a long interval, fired up again with a hope of liberty.

SOURCE: *The Orations of Marcus Tullius Cicero*. Translated by C. D. Yonge. London: Henry G. Bohn. 1852.

JULIUS AGRICOLA

TO HIS SOLDIERS IN BRITAIN
(84 A.D.)

Though a renowned orator himself in his time, none of the speeches of the Roman historian Tacitus (c. 56–118 A.D.) have survived; instead, we have the speeches he wrote as a biographer and historian. In *Agricola*, Tacitus writes the story of his father-in-law, a former consul, who as a governor battled, conquered and administered the wild tribes of Britain, extending the Roman Empire as far as Scotland. Agricola was born in 37 A.D. and died in 93.

<hr/>

[Tacitus's narrative:] *While the enemy's line was thus forming, Agricola, though his men were in excellent spirits and could hardly be kept within the entrenchments, judged it well still further to enflame their zeal by the following harangue:*

Fellow-soldiers, this is now the seventh year in which, under the leadership of imperial Rome, and by the help of your constancy and valor, we have jointly fought as conquerors of Britain. Many have been our campaigns and battles, all calling either for courage against the foe or for endurance and toil in combating the very forces of nature; but in none have I had occasion to repent me of my men, nor you of your leader. Thus together we have passed the limits which bounded former generals and former armies, and on the remotest shore of Britain, where only rumor and hearsay had penetrated before, have planted our camps and our arms.

Britain is ours by discovery and conquest. How often, when morass or mountain or river blocked our march, have I not heard from your bravest the impatient cry for the enemy and the battle-field. Behold them now, driven forth from their hiding. The longed for moment has come, and valor need chafe no longer. As victors all is in your favor; defeated, all would be against you.

All the triumph and glory of our advance—the distance we have surmounted, the forests we have pierced, the rivers we have crossed—encouragements as these are to us today, would be so many perils added to our flight. We are inferior both in knowledge of the country and in supply of provisions; but our courage and our swords make us the masters. For myself, it has long been my prin-ciple that neither for general nor army is there safety except in pressing forward. An honorable death, we know, is better than a life of shame, but here safety and honor go together; nor would it be an inglorious fate to have fallen on the spot where the earth and nature alike find their limit.

Those now arrayed before you were a strange and untried peo-ple, I would urge you by the example of other armies; as it is, you have but to count your own trophies, to ask your own eyes. These are the men who, last year attacking a single legion by night, were disarmed by your shouts; these are the Britons who are readiest at flight, and who for this reason have survived so long. For as when forcing a road through woods and thickets we found ourselves attacked by the bolder animals, while the very sound of our tread would scatter the timid and sluggish; even so the boldest of the Britons have already fallen; what remains is but a quaking rabble, whose flight even now necessity alone has stayed. Numbed by des-peration and dire fear, their ranks are transfixed to this spot, which shall be for you the scene of a splendid and memorable victory.

Put an end now to your toils; crown fifty years with a day of glory, and let Rome witness that, if the war has been long and Britain apt to rebel, the fault has not lain with the army.

[Tacitus's narrative:] *The excitement of the troops could hardly be kept in bounds even while Agricola was speaking, and no sooner had he ended than with a burst of ardor they flew to arms. The eager surging throng were marshaled by Agricola in the following order: the foot-soldiers of the auxil-iaries, numbering eight thousand, formed a stout phalanx in the center, while their cavalry, to the number of three thousand, were spread over the wings. The legions were stationed in front of the entrenchment, that the glory of victory might be enhanced by the sparing of Roman blood, whilst their aid would be in reserve in case of a repulse. The British force meanwhile, the more to strike terror by a show of strength, had been drawn up on the heights in such a way that from the front rank, stationed on level ground, the whole seemed to rise in unbroken curve over the hill-side. The plain between the armies was filled with the clatter of hurrying charioteers. Agricola, fearing, when he saw the great superiority of the enemy in numbers, that he might be attacked at once in front and on the flank, extended his own line, though at the risk of unduly weakening it. Hopeful by nature, he was not to be driven from his purpose by difficulties, and, disregarding the general advice to call up the legions, he dismounted and took his place on foot before the banner of the auxiliaries.*

SOURCE: Publius Cornelius Tacitus. *The Agricola of Tacitus*. Anonymous translator. London: Kegan Paul, Trench and Company. 1885.

SOURCES & SELECTED
BIBLIOGRAPHY

Kenneth J. Atchity. *The Classical Roman Reader*. New York: Henry Holt. 1997.

Edward Capps. *From Homer to Theocritus: A Manual of Greek Literature*. New York: Charles Scribner's Sons. 1901.

Cicero. *The Orations of Marcus Tullius Cicero*. Translated by C. D. Yonge. London: Henry G. Bohn. 1852.

Demosthenes. *All the Orations of Demosthenes: Pronounced to Excite the Athenians Against Philip, King of Macedon*. Translated by Thomas Leland. London: W. Johnston. 1757.

Herodotus. *The Histories*. Translated by Aubrey de Selincourt. Revised by A. R. Burn. Harmondsworth, England: Penguin. 1984.

R. C. Jebb. *The Attic Orators from Antiphon to Isaeos*. Volume 2. London: Macmillian and Company. 1876.

H. D. F. Kitto. *The Greeks*. Harmondsworth, England: Penguin. 1973.

Bernard Knox. *Backing into the Future: The Classical Tradition and Its Renewal*. New York: W. W. Norton and Company. 1994.

Guy Carleton Lee. *Orators of Ancient Rome*. New York: G. P. Putnam's Sons. 1900.

————. *Orators of Ancient Greece*. New York: G. P. Putnam's Sons. 1900.

————. *The World's Orators*. University Edition. New York: G. P. Putnam's Sons. 1900.

Livy. *The History of Rome by Titus Livius*. Translated by D. Spillan and Cyrus Edmonds. London: Henry G. Bohn. 1849.

Perseus Digital Library. http://www.perseus.tufts.edu/hopper/

Plato. *The Dialogues of Plato: Translated into English, with Analyses and Introductions*. Volume 2. Translated by Benjamin Jowett. New York: Scribner, Armstrong and Company. 1874.

Plutarch. *Fall of the Roman Republic: Six Lives by Plutarch*. Translated by Rex Warner. Harmondsworth, England: Penguin. 1983.

———. *The Lives of the Nobel Grecians and Romans*. Translated by John Dryden. Revised by Arthur Hugh Clough. New York: Modern Library (Random House). 1932.

———. *The Rise and Fall of Athens: Nine Greek Lives by Plutarch*. Translated by Ian Scott-Kilvert. Harmondsworth, England: Penguin. 1979.

Marcus Fabius Quintilianus. *The Institutio Oratoria of Quintilian with an English Translation by H. E. Butler*. London: William Heineman. 1933.

A. N. W. Saunders. *Greek Political Oratory*. Harmondsworth, England: Penguin. 1970.

Catherine Steel. *Roman Oratory*. Cambridge: Cambridge University Press for the Classical Association. 2006.

Publius Cornelius Tacitus. *The Agricola of Tacitus*. Anonymous translator. London: Kegan Paul, Trench and Company. 1885.

———. *Complete Works of Tacitus*. Edited by Moses Hadas. New York: Random House. 1942.

Thucydides. *The History of the Peloponnesian War*. Translated by R. W. Livingstone. Oxford: Oxford University Press. 1943.

———. *The History of the Peloponnesian War by Thucydides*. Translated by Henry Dale. London: Henry G. Bohn. 1849.

———. *Thucydides Translated into English, With Introduction, Marginal Analysis, Notes, and Indices*. Translated by Benjamin Jowett. Oxford at the Clarendon Press. 1881.

John Selby Watson. *Sallust, Florus, and Velleius Paterculus*. London: Henry G. Bohn. 1852.

Xenophon. *The Works of Xenophon: Hellenica, Books I & II, and Anabasis*. Translated by H. G. Dakyns. London: Macmillan and Company. 1890.

———. *Xenophon's Anabasis: Books I–IV*. Notes and vocabulary by Maurice W. Mather and Joseph William Hewitt. Norman, Oklahoma: University of Oklahoma Press. 1979.

DOVER·THRIFT·EDITIONS

FICTION

ADVENTURES OF HUCKLEBERRY FINN, Mark Twain. (0-486-28061-6)

THE AWAKENING, Kate Chopin. (0-486-27786-0)

A CHRISTMAS CAROL, Charles Dickens. (0-486-26865-9)

FRANKENSTEIN, Mary Shelley. (0-486-28211-2)

HEART OF DARKNESS, Joseph Conrad. (0-486-26464-5)

PRIDE AND PREJUDICE, Jane Austen. (0-486-28473-5)

THE SCARLET LETTER, Nathaniel Hawthorne. (0-486-28048-9)

THE ADVENTURES OF TOM SAWYER, Mark Twain. (0-486-40077-8)

ALICE'S ADVENTURES IN WONDERLAND, Lewis Carroll. (0-486-27543-4)

THE CALL OF THE WILD, Jack London. (0-486-26472-6)

CRIME AND PUNISHMENT, Fyodor Dostoyevsky. Translated by Constance Garnett. (0-486-41587-2)

DRACULA, Bram Stoker. (0-486-41109-5)

ETHAN FROME, Edith Wharton. (0-486-26690-7)

FLATLAND, Edwin A. Abbott. (0-486-27263-X)

GREAT AMERICAN SHORT STORIES, Edited by Paul Negri. (0-486-42119-8)

GREAT EXPECTATIONS, Charles Dickens. (0-486-41586-4)

JANE EYRE, Charlotte Brontë. (0-486-42449-9)

THE JUNGLE, Upton Sinclair. (0-486-41923-1)

THE METAMORPHOSIS AND OTHER STORIES, Franz Kafka. (0-486-29030-1)

THE ODYSSEY, Homer. (0-486-40654-7)

THE PICTURE OF DORIAN GRAY, Oscar Wilde. (0-486-27807-7)

SIDDHARTHA, Hermann Hesse. (0-486-40653-9)

THE STRANGE CASE OF DR. JEKYLL AND MR. HYDE, Robert Louis Stevenson. (0-486-26688-5)

A TALE OF TWO CITIES, Charles Dickens. (0-486-40651-2)

WUTHERING HEIGHTS, Emily Brontë. (0-486-29256-8)

ANNA KARENINA, Leo Tolstoy. Translated by Louise and Aylmer Maude. (0-486-43796-5)

AROUND THE WORLD IN EIGHTY DAYS, Jules Verne. (0-486-41111-7)

THE BROTHERS KARAMAZOV, Fyodor Dostoyevsky. Translated by Constance Garnett. (0-486-43791-4)

DOVER·THRIFT·EDITIONS

CANDIDE, Voltaire. Edited by Francois-Marie Arouet. (0-486-26689-3)

DAISY MILLER, Henry James. (0-486-28773-4)

DAVID COPPERFIELD, Charles Dickens. (0-486-43665-9)

DUBLINERS, James Joyce. (0-486-26870-5)

EMMA, Jane Austen. (0-486-40648-2)

THE GIFT OF THE MAGI AND OTHER SHORT STORIES, O. Henry. (0-486-27061-0)

THE GOLD-BUG AND OTHER TALES, Edgar Allan Poe. (0-486-26875-6)

GREAT SHORT SHORT STORIES, Edited by Paul Negri. (0-486-44098-2)

GULLIVER'S TRAVELS, Jonathan Swift. (0-486-29273-8)

HARD TIMES, Charles Dickens. (0-486-41920-7)

THE HOUND OF THE BASKERVILLES, Arthur Conan Doyle. (0-486-28214-7)

THE ILIAD, Homer. (0-486-40883-3)

MOBY-DICK, Herman Melville. (0-486-43215-7)

MY ÁNTONIA, Willa Cather. (0-486-28240-6)

NORTHANGER ABBEY, Jane Austen. (0-486-41412-4)

NOT WITHOUT LAUGHTER, Langston Hughes. (0-486-45448-7)

OLIVER TWIST, Charles Dickens. (0-486-42453-7)

PERSUASION, Jane Austen. (0-486-29555-9)

THE PHANTOM OF THE OPERA, Gaston Leroux. (0-486-43458-3)

A PORTRAIT OF THE ARTIST AS A YOUNG MAN, James Joyce. (0-486-28050-0)

PUDD'NHEAD WILSON, Mark Twain. (0-486-40885-X)

THE RED BADGE OF COURAGE, Stephen Crane. (0-486-26465-3)

THE SCARLET PIMPERNEL, Baroness Orczy. (0-486-42122-8)

SENSE AND SENSIBILITY, Jane Austen. (0-486-29049-2)

SILAS MARNER, George Eliot. (0-486-29246-0)

TESS OF THE D'URBERVILLES, Thomas Hardy. (0-486-41589-9)

THE TIME MACHINE, H. G. Wells. (0-486-28472-7)

TREASURE ISLAND, Robert Louis Stevenson. (0-486-27559-0)

THE TURN OF THE SCREW, Henry James. (0-486-26684-2)

UNCLE TOM'S CABIN, Harriet Beecher Stowe. (0-486-44028-1)

THE WAR OF THE WORLDS, H. G. Wells. (0-486-29506-0)

THE WORLD'S GREATEST SHORT STORIES, Edited by James Daley. (0-486-44716-2)

THE AGE OF INNOCENCE, Edith Wharton. (0-486-29803-5)

AGNES GREY, Anne Brontë. (0-486-45121-6)

AT FAULT, Kate Chopin. (0-486-46133-5)

THE AUTOBIOGRAPHY OF AN EX-COLORED MAN, James Weldon Johnson. (0-486-28512-X)

BARTLEBY AND BENITO CERENO, Herman Melville. (0-486-26473-4)

BEOWULF, Translated by R. K. Gordon. (0-486-27264-8)

CIVIL WAR STORIES, Ambrose Bierce. (0-486-28038-1)

A CONNECTICUT YANKEE IN KING ARTHUR'S COURT, Mark Twain. (0-486-41591-0)

THE DEERSLAYER, James Fenimore Cooper. (0-486-46136-X)

DEMIAN, Hermann Hesse. (0-486-41413-2)

FAR FROM THE MADDING CROWD, Thomas Hardy. (0-486-45684-6)

FAVORITE FATHER BROWN STORIES, G. K. Chesterton. (0-486-27545-0)

GREAT HORROR STORIES, Edited by John Grafton. Introduction by Mike Ashley. (0-486-46143-2)

GREAT RUSSIAN SHORT STORIES, Edited by Paul Negri. (0-486-42992-X)

GREAT SHORT STORIES BY AMERICAN WOMEN, Edited by Candace Ward. (0-486-28776-9)

GRIMM'S FAIRY TALES, Jacob and Wilhelm Grimm. (0-486-45656-0)

HUMOROUS STORIES AND SKETCHES, Mark Twain. (0-486-29279-7)

THE HUNCHBACK OF NOTRE DAME, Victor Hugo. Translated by A. L. Alger. (0-486-45242-5)

THE INVISIBLE MAN, H. G. Wells. (0-486-27071-8)

THE ISLAND OF DR. MOREAU, H. G. Wells. (0-486-29027-1)

A JOURNAL OF THE PLAGUE YEAR, Daniel Defoe. (0-486-41919-3)

JOURNEY TO THE CENTER OF THE EARTH, Jules Verne. (0-486-44088-5)

KIM, Rudyard Kipling. (0-486-44508-9)

THE LAST OF THE MOHICANS, James Fenimore Cooper. (0-486-42678-5)

THE LEGEND OF SLEEPY HOLLOW AND OTHER STORIES, Washington Irving. (0-486-46658-2)

LILACS AND OTHER STORIES, Kate Chopin. (0-486-44095-8)

MANSFIELD PARK, Jane Austen. (0-486-41585-6)

THE MAYOR OF CASTERBRIDGE, Thomas Hardy. (0-486-43749-3)

DOVER · THRIFT · EDITIONS

THE MYSTERIOUS STRANGER AND OTHER STORIES, Mark Twain.
(0-486-27069-6)

NOTES FROM THE UNDERGROUND, Fyodor Dostoyevsky. (0-486-27053-X)

O PIONEERS!, Willa Cather. (0-486-27785-2)

AN OCCURRENCE AT OWL CREEK BRIDGE AND OTHER STORIES,
Ambrose Bierce. (0-486-46657-4)

THE OLD CURIOSITY SHOP, Charles Dickens. (0-486-42679-3)

THE OPEN BOAT AND OTHER STORIES, Stephen Crane. (0-486-27547-7)

ROBINSON CRUSOE, Daniel Defoe. (0-486-40427-7)

THIS SIDE OF PARADISE, F. Scott Fitzgerald. (0-486-28999-0)

THE THREE MUSKETEERS, Alexandre Dumas. (0-486-45681-1)

TWENTY THOUSAND LEAGUES UNDER THE SEA, Jules Verne. (0-486-44849-5)

WHITE FANG, Jack London. (0-486-26968-X)

WHITE NIGHTS AND OTHER STORIES, Fyodor Dostoyevsky. (0-486-46948-4)

NONFICTION

GREAT SPEECHES, Abraham Lincoln. (0-486-26872-1)

WISDOM OF THE BUDDHA, Edited by F. Max Müller. (0-486-41120-6)

NARRATIVE OF SOJOURNER TRUTH, Sojourner Truth. (0-486-29899-X)

THE TRIAL AND DEATH OF SOCRATES, Plato. (0-486-27066-1)

WIT AND WISDOM OF THE AMERICAN PRESIDENTS, Edited by Joslyn Pine.
(0-486-41427-2)

GREAT SPEECHES BY AFRICAN AMERICANS, Edited by James Daley.
(0-486-44761-8)

INTERIOR CASTLE, St. Teresa of Avila. Edited and Translated by E. Allison
Peers. (0-486-46145-9)

GREAT SPEECHES BY AMERICAN WOMEN, Edited by James Daley.
(0-486-46141-6)

ON LIBERTY, John Stuart Mill. (0-486-42130-9)

MEDITATIONS, Marcus Aurelius. (0-486-29823-X)

THE SOULS OF BLACK FOLK, W.E.B. DuBois. (0-486-28041-1)

GREAT SPEECHES BY NATIVE AMERICANS, Edited by Bob Blaisdell.
(0-486-41122-2)

WIT AND WISDOM FROM POOR RICHARD'S ALMANACK, Benjamin Franklin.
(0-486-40891-4)

DOVER·THRIFT·EDITIONS

THE AUTOBIOGRAPHY OF BENJAMIN FRANKLIN, Benjamin Franklin. (0-486-29073-5)

OSCAR WILDE'S WIT AND WISDOM, Oscar Wilde. (0-486-40146-4)

THE WIT AND WISDOM OF ABRAHAM LINCOLN, Abraham Lincoln. Edited by Bob Blaisdell. (0-486-44097-4)

ON THE ORIGIN OF SPECIES, Charles Darwin. (0-486-45006-6)

SIX GREAT DIALOGUES, Plato. Translated by Benjamin Jowett. (0-486-45465-7)

NATURE AND OTHER ESSAYS, Ralph Waldo Emerson. (0-486-46947-6)

THE COMMUNIST MANIFESTO AND OTHER REVOLUTIONARY WRITINGS, Edited by Bob Blaisdell. (0-486-42465-0)

THE CONFESSIONS OF ST. AUGUSTINE, St. Augustine. (0-486-42466-9)

THE WIT AND WISDOM OF MARK TWAIN, Mark Twain. (0-486-40664-4)

LIFE ON THE MISSISSIPPI, Mark Twain. (0-486-41426-4)

BEYOND GOOD AND EVIL, Friedrich Nietzsche. (0-486-29868-X)

CIVIL DISOBEDIENCE AND OTHER ESSAYS, Henry David Thoreau. (0-486-27563-9)

A MODEST PROPOSAL AND OTHER SATIRICAL WORKS, Jonathan Swift. (0-486-28759-9)

UTOPIA, Sir Thomas More. (0-486-29583-4)

GREAT SPEECHES, Franklin Delano Roosevelt. (0-486-40894-9)

WALDEN; OR, LIFE IN THE WOODS, Henry David Thoreau. (0-486-28495-6)

UP FROM SLAVERY, Booker T. Washington. (0-486-28738-6)

DARK NIGHT OF THE SOUL, St. John of the Cross. (0-486-42693-9)

GREEK AND ROMAN LIVES, Plutarch. Translated by John Dryden. Revised and Edited by Arthur Hugh Clough. (0-486-44576-3)

WOMEN'S WIT AND WISDOM, Edited by Susan L. Rattiner. (0-486-41123-0)

MUSIC, Edited by Herb Galewitz. (0-486-41596-1)

INCIDENTS IN THE LIFE OF A SLAVE GIRL, Harriet Jacobs. (0-486-41931-2)

THE LIFE OF OLAUDAH EQUIANO, Olaudah Equiano. (0-486-40661-X)

THE DECLARATION OF INDEPENDENCE AND OTHER GREAT DOCUMENTS OF AMERICAN HISTORY, Edited by John Grafton. (0-486-41124-9)

THE PRINCE, Niccolò Machiavelli. (0-486-27274-5)

WOMAN IN THE NINETEENTH CENTURY, Margaret Fuller. (0-486-40662-8)

SELF-RELIANCE AND OTHER ESSAYS, Ralph Waldo Emerson. (0-486-27790-9)

COMMON SENSE, Thomas Paine. (0-486-29602-4)

DOVER · THRIFT · EDITIONS

THE REPUBLIC, Plato. (0-486-41121-4)

POETICS, Aristotle. (0-486-29577-X)

THE DEVIL'S DICTIONARY, Ambrose Bierce. (0-486-27542-6)

NARRATIVE OF THE LIFE OF FREDERICK DOUGLASS, Frederick Douglass. (0-486-28499-9)

GREAT ENGLISH ESSAYS, Edited by Bob Blaisdell. (0-486-44082-6)

THE KORAN, Translated by J. M. Rodwell. (0-486-44569-0)

28 GREAT INAUGURAL ADDRESSES, Edited by John Grafton and James Daley. (0-486-44621-2)

WHEN I WAS A SLAVE, Edited by Norman R. Yetman. (0-486-42070-1)

THE IMITATION OF CHRIST, Thomas à Kempis. Translated by Aloysius Croft and Harold Bolton. (0-486-43185-1)

PLAYS

ANTIGONE, Sophocles. (0-486-27804-2)

AS YOU LIKE IT, William Shakespeare. (0-486-40432-3)

CYRANO DE BERGERAC, Edmond Rostand. (0-486-41119-2)

A DOLL'S HOUSE, Henrik Ibsen. (0-486-27062-9)

DR. FAUSTUS, Christopher Marlowe. (0-486-28208-2)

FIVE COMIC ONE-ACT PLAYS, Anton Chekhov. (0-486-40887-6)

FIVE GREAT COMEDIES, William Shakespeare. (0-486-44086-9)

FIVE GREAT GREEK TRAGEDIES, Sophocles, Euripides and Aeschylus. (0-486-43620-9)

FOUR GREAT HISTORIES, William Shakespeare. (0-486-44629-8)

FOUR GREAT RUSSIAN PLAYS, Anton Chekhov, Nikolai Gogol, Maxim Gorky, and Ivan Turgenev. (0-486-43472-9)

FOUR GREAT TRAGEDIES, William Shakespeare. (0-486-44083-4)

GHOSTS, Henrik Ibsen. (0-486-29852-3)

HAMLET, William Shakespeare. (0-486-27278-8)

HENRY V, William Shakespeare. (0-486-42887-7)

AN IDEAL HUSBAND, Oscar Wilde. (0-486-41423-X)

THE IMPORTANCE OF BEING EARNEST, Oscar Wilde. (0-486-26478-5)

JULIUS CAESAR, William Shakespeare. (0-486-26876-4)

KING LEAR, William Shakespeare. (0-486-28058-6)